MAN
AND LAW OF PLANET EARTH

BlueRose ONE
Stories Matter
NewDelhi • London

BLUEROSE PUBLISHERS
India | U.K.

Copyright © Kalptaru Anil S Thakkar 2025

All rights reserved by author. No part of this publication may be reproduced, stored in a retrieval system or transmitted in any form or by any means, electronic, mechanical, photocopying, recording or otherwise, without the prior permission of the author. Although every precaution has been taken to verify the accuracy of the information contained herein, the publisher assume no responsibility for any errors or omissions. No liability is assumed for damages that may result from the use of information contained within.

BlueRose Publishers takes no responsibility for any damages, losses, or liabilities that may arise from the use or misuse of the information, products, or services provided in this publication.

BlueRose ONE
Stories Matter
New Delhi • London

For permissions requests or inquiries regarding this publication, please contact:

BLUEROSE PUBLISHERS
www.BlueRoseONE.com
info@bluerosepublishers.com
+91 8882 898 898
+4407342408967

ISBN: 978-93-6783-043-7

Cover design: Daksh
Typesetting: Tanya Raj Upadhyay

First Edition: January 2025

INTRODUCTION

MAN & Law of Planet

Question from Sakshi Ji:

What is the impact of Vastu Shastra at the national level?

Answer:

Vastu Shastra holds immense significance not only at an individual level but also at a national scale, influencing the rise and fall of nations. Its principles apply universally, and when ignored, can lead to destruction on a larger stage. For instance, the collapse of Bangladesh serves as an example of the impact of disregarding Vastu principles.

On a daily basis, the influence of Vastu can be observed. Every day at 10:30 AM, a subtle yet profound offering occurs as a result of the historical timing of India's first flag hoisting on August 15, 1947. This act, tied to the nation's collective energy, symbolizes an offering of Rajoguna (passion-driven energy) from individuals, which gradually depletes mental resilience. Over time, this contributes to mass frustration, mental instability, and national upheaval, similar to disputes seen in nuclear families—different stories, but the root cause is the same.

In Vastu Shastra, concrete constructions are discouraged, as they conflict with the natural principles of Sanatan Sanskriti (eternal culture). When these laws are ignored, the consequences are evident at both personal and national levels. The shift from "It's my duty" to "It's my life" has disrupted the foundational values that once upheld societal harmony.

The challenges faced by nations today are reflections of unresolved individual struggles, magnified on a larger scale. While the current ruling party has attempted to address these issues over the past decade, many unresolved challenges remain, including international conflicts. It's worth noting that India, as a nation, is still under a symbolic 99-year lease linked to British rule.

Historically, foreign powers such as the Dutch, French, Portuguese, Americans and later the British arrived via sea routes under the guise of trade and established their dominance, often by dismantling the native systems. Even before them, during the Mughal era and earlier, the crisis of leadership and governance was evident. The period of Chanakya offers lessons, where he has denied the king, " RAJOGUNA".

Vastu Shastra, as ancient Rishis proclaimed, permits only the king to build structures, with subjects residing in those constructed under his guidance. When these principles are violated, the influence of Mayasur—symbolizing chaos and destruction—is inevitable.

As we continue to celebrate Independence Day, we must reflect on these lessons from history. Recognizing and adhering to the principles of Vastu can restore harmony and prevent further internal and external crises for individuals and the nation alike.

Hari Om!

Question:

What is the root cause of human suffering in the current era? We often hear that life was better during the time of our forefathers.

Asked by the Manager of BRP to Swamiji

Swamiji's Response:

The root cause of human suffering can be traced to the very moment of birth. During delivery, the infant often experiences a dent in their skull caused by the obstetrician or gynecologist assisting in the delivery process. This initial trauma is the reason the baby cries upon entering the world—it not only causes physical pain but also creates a subtle, lifelong impact that connects to the mother, the child's first Devta (giver).

This physical imprint on the skull, combined with other physiological influences, sets the stage for the individual's struggles throughout life. For the first ten days after birth, the baby also absorbs residual sperm particles from the womb that are attracted to the protective sheath provided by the mother. This sperm imprint, combined with subtle physiological and psychological impacts, leads to a recurring sense of inner conflict, as if the individual is constantly grappling with an internal dialogue between "yes" and "no."

Over time, these residual imprints attract further impurities from the external environment, such as menstrual discharges or other female-specific secretions. These layers accumulate, creating additional pressures on the individual's psyche, often leading to restless thoughts or behaviors. In spiritual terms, these imprints symbolize layers of unresolved energies— "dent upon dent"—that weigh down the individual, making life seem burdensome.

Relief and Traditional Remedies:

In Indian tradition, specific rituals and practices are prescribed to counteract these effects. On the 10th day after birth, a specific purification ritual is performed. Traditionally, the child is bathed and then carried into the courtyard by the younger brother-in-law of the mother (a bachelor), who wields an arrow in his left hand. During this ritual, the impurities are symbolically cleansed, and the individual takes a vow to protect the child throughout their life. This practice is mentioned in Valmiki Ramayana and is part of the 16 Sanskaras prescribed in Indian scriptures.

These Sanskaras—starting from conception (Garbhadhana) and extending through rituals like Annaprashana (first feeding), Yagnopavita (sacred thread ceremony), and so on—serve to purify and uplift the individual throughout their life. Even after death, these rites are continued for 16 days (known as Sutak) to ensure that any missed rituals during life are fulfilled, preventing difficulties in the next birth.

Similarly, the first 10 days after birth, known as Vriddhi, are marked by seclusion and protection for the newborn to preserve their purity and individuality.

Through these ancient practices, families aim to safeguard the child from lifelong burdens and ensure a harmonious existence.

Hari Om!

TABLE OF CONTENTS

BEYOND TIME ZONE 1

QUESTIONNAIRE ON DIABETES 36

REWIRING OF MIND 59

QUESTIONEIR ON VASTU : CHALLENGE OF
THE DEMON 80

BEYOND TIME ZONE

Dr. Jyotsna Singh:

Good evening, everyone. Today, we are honored to have Swami Ji with us, a person who has accomplished so much in his life that words fall short to describe him. Swami Ji will sit by a tree near the Narmada River and help us experience the essence of the river and its divine beauty. Please approach this session with an open mind and heart, so you can truly feel the peace and serenity being shared. In just two minutes of listening, I have been deeply mesmerized, and I believe you too will understand and feel its profound impact.

I deeply thank Swami Ji for gracing our platform with his presence and for taking out such valuable time to share his ideology with us, particularly for the benefit of the youth and children. Through his words, he will beautifully convey the wisdom and knowledge he has gained throughout his life. I urge everyone to spare some time and listen to him, as this session, this webinar, has the potential to bring significant changes to your life. So, please join me in welcoming Swami Ji. Swami Ji, we are eager to hear from you. Thank you.

Swami Ji:

What you see in front of you is Bhim Talab, a place of penance by Bhim during the Dwapara Yuga. This pond was created during that era, and the temple you see here is the Ram Janaki Temple. Behind this temple, Bhim established a Shivalaya. <u>dedicated to Ram Ji and Janaki Mata.</u> This site is situated on the southern bank of the Narmada River, traditionally referred to as the "bank of ancestors," while the northern bank is known as the "bank of gods."

This ancient Shivalaya, Kedareshwar Mahadev, is mentioned in the *Skanda Purana* in the Reva Khand. "Reva" is another name for the Narmada River. The banyan tree you see here shelters a hut that was recently constructed. Although it is still unfinished, it is part of the ashram where saints and sages reside. Behind the ashram, you can see a cow shelter, which serves the cows of the local village.

The village, Sondaliya, is located approximately 2.5 kilometers away. It belongs to the Narmada district, which was established only two years ago; before that, it was part of Bharuch district in Gujarat. This Ram

Janki temple here and its ashram have existed for 25 years, and it took nearly the same amount of time to bring electricity here from the village. The cost of installing electricity poles alone was 30 lakh rupees, as it is situated in such a remote area.

The atmosphere here is entirely free from pollution, offering a tranquil and serene environment. Pilgrims undertaking the Narmada Parikrama, referred to as Jagat Bhagat, frequently visit this place, as do other sadhus and saints. The ashram provides arrangements for their meals (*prasadi*) and overnight stays. For seekers (*sadhaks*) wishing to stay longer, accommodations, including smaller rooms and larger halls, have been built.

You can see this beautiful view of the Narmada here. Now, let us delve into the topic of our discussion. As you mentioned earlier, some introductions were provided. I would like to make a slight correction to them. My name is Swami Kalpataru, and I received My initiation into Karma Yoga Sanyas in 1977. Our Guru Maharaj, Swami Satyanand Saraswati, founded the Bihar School of Yoga in 1963 in Munger, Bihar, by the banks of the Ganges. The ashram there is known as Ganga Darshan Ashram.

However, we received our personal initiation from Guru Maharaj in 1977 in Raipur, which is now the capital of Chhattisgarh. In 1975, My parents also took initiation from Guru Maharaj. They have now passed away (*become Dev*). My younger brother and sister also took initiation in Karma Yoga Sanyas but chose the path of family life through marriage.

For Me, the two choices were either to serve the country by joining the military or to embrace sanyas and spread dharma. I found the latter more suitable and chose this path. Although I studied in a convent school, My spiritual studies included subjects like astrology, rituals (*Yantra Shastra*), the *Upanishads*, and the *Puranas*.

After taking sanyas, I traveled across India three times and even undertook a 9,700-kilometer bicycle expedition along the coastline. Regarding the earlier introduction, I would like to clarify that (while this Kedareshwar Mahadev is an ancient establishment). I'm neither the founder of the Munger Ashram nor its secretary.

This is a clarification. The current Mahant of the ashram is Swami Niranjananand Saraswati Ji. A Mahant is the officer or head of the ashram, and this ashram has other branches. Beyond Bharuch, there are districts like Vadodara, Kheda, and Nadiad. In Kheda district, there is a village called Heernch. In MATAR tehsil there, you will find the Gyan Vihar Ashram, where yoga classes are also conducted. Discourses on Patanjali Yoga and the *Yoga Sutras* of Patanjali are organized there as well.

This was part of my introduction. The southern belt of the Narmada River, which you see here, is considered the "bank of ancestors," while the northern bank is known as the "bank of gods," as described in the Puranas. This ashram has steps leading down to the ghat. There is also a hut where I have an *aasan* (seat).

I will take you to the hut, though it may not be very clear due to network issues in this area. The signal is more stable near the hut, so please continue with your questions. My gratitude to all the listeners for their efforts, and special thanks to Vajpayee Ji. It is remarkable that they visited this ashram, located in such a remote and tranquil setting, just last week. Their visit has made this session possible.

I 'm happy to share some of the wisdom imparted by our Gurus. Hari Om. Are you able to hear me ?

Dr. Jyotsna Singh:

Yes, Swami Ji, we can hear you very clearly.

Swami Ji:

Good, good. Now let's address your questions.

Dr. Jyotsna Singh:

Yes, Swami Ji, we are ready with the questions.

Swami Ji:

All right, the introduction is now complete.

Dr. Jyotsna Singh:

Yes, indeed. Please take your seat first.

Swami Ji:

There is no issue. We are entering the hut now. Let me show it to you—it is a simple one. There is a *chauki* inside for aasan. Look, this is the entryway. This is where we are right now. It's small but sufficient. We arranged everything here.

Here is the window, and this is the view from it. This is the table we arranged, which they referred to as a laptop table. With this, I can continue the discussion with you. Now, please go ahead with your questions.

Dr. Jyotsna Singh:

Swami Ji, as you mentioned, you have gained many experiences in your life. What knowledge can you share, from children to the elderly, that can help us make our lives successful and bring awareness? Many people lack awareness, even if they achieve success or wealth. On the other hand, there are some who continuously struggle. What should we do to align our mind, body, and soul? Please explain in simple language so that we understand *why we are here on this Earth.* This is a profound question.

Swami Ji:

Very, very good question. If you are on this Earth, why are you here? This is indeed the core of your question. If you are born on this planet, the first step is to understand the demand of planet Earth itself.

Consider the movement of Earth—not just through astrology or mathematics but in a straightforward way. Earth rotates and revolves. Morning turns into evening, and a year is completed in 365 days. This is because the Earth orbits its source of light, the Sun, which sustains life here. The concept of circumambulation in our Sanatan culture (often called Hindu culture) originates from this: circling around one's source of light.

Now, what is the *Yama* (law) of Earth? What are its principles? You can observe the Earth's impact on your body through something as common as fingerprints. Everyone is familiar with fingerprints, especially since Aadhaar cards were introduced in India. Your fingerprint is unique, just like the vein patterns on a Banyan tree's leaves. This connection between the Earth's movements and its imprints is evident both in human fingerprints and in the natural world.

When you live your life aligned with the Yama, the law of nature, you find harmony. Acting against these natural laws leads to struggle. Swimming against the current increases difficulties. This alignment is what we call *Dharma*. Dharma means law, and when this law is implemented, it becomes *Niyam* (discipline).

The *Ashtanga Yoga Sutras*, widely propagated by Baba Ramdev and others, emphasize these principles: *Yama* (laws) and *Niyama* (disciplines). According to the Dharma of Earth, you are born into your mother's womb. While in the womb, your life begins to take shape, influenced by external sounds and interactions.

Dr. Jyotsna, as a neuroscientist, you know that a human's entire life starts forming in the womb. The fetus interacts with its surroundings—not just recognizing family members like the father, uncle, or sister, but also interacting with the voices of animals, birds, and even trees. These early interactions create imprints.

Every individual is unique, just as no two leaves on the same tree are identical. Each human being has a distinct nature and personality. Throughout life, a person continues to operate within the imprints formed during their time in the womb. For example, if a pregnant mother witnesses a bullfight, the child might carry an imprint of that aggression. It may manifest differently, but it influences their comfort zones and career choices.

This is why children often follow the professions of their parents. For instance, doctors' children may also become doctors, even if in different specializations. The same happens in fields like the film industry or cricket, where family legacies are common.

To live a fulfilling life, one must understand the Dharma of Earth and align with it. When you live according to these natural laws, struggles diminish. This concept has been explained in various scriptures and is even reflected in ancient Indian texts. If we consider India, we find that our ancestors, whom we call Rishis, were very deliberate in naming this land. They chose the name *Bharat*. In Sanskrit, *Bha* signifies knowledge, so Bharat means a land immersed in knowledge. Similarly, the Sun is referred to as *Bhaskar*, the giver of knowledge. The word *Dhi* means intelligence, and intelligence is also derived from the Sun.

Let us now talk about the river Narmada. Its flow begins at Amarkantak in the east and ends in the Arabian Sea, passing through places like Bharuch and Ankleshwar. Narmada is considered a river of knowledge and is referred to as the daughter of Lord Shankar. There is a belief that she was born from the sweat of Lord Shiva. A related story can be found in the writings of Adi Shankaracharya, who composed the *Narmada Ashtakam*. In this, he describes the river poetically:

"Sabbindu Sindhu Sukhal Tarang Bhring Ranji Dam."

Here, *Sabbindu Sindhu* refers to the droplets (Bindu) of sweat from Lord Shiva that form an ocean of knowledge. This poetic representation conveys that Lord Shiva, or Mahadev, is devoid of ignorance (*Tamas*). He is the embodiment of knowledge, and Narmada, born from his sweat, symbolizes this profound wisdom.

Our Rishis have beautifully articulated these ideas in the scriptures, emphasizing the importance of knowledge. The word *Bha*, as used in Bharat, reflects this immersion in wisdom. In India, the focus has always been on understanding and living in harmony with the laws of planet Earth.

The term *Sanatan Dharma* is often discussed as eternal. But what is *Sanatan*? It means ancient. It cannot be compared to any religion because it is beyond time and predates any organized faith. The most ancient Dharma is the law of nature, the very principles that govern life on Earth. Living against these laws creates challenges and struggles.

Religious activities—prayers, rituals, and offerings—are important, but they are not sufficient on their own. In daily life, one must remain aware and ensure they do not violate the laws of nature. For example, even basic activities like wearing clothes, cooking food, or drinking water have guidelines in our scriptures. Our Rishis have written extensively on these topics, such as

Kanchuki Shastra (the art of clothing) and *Paak Shastra* (the art of cooking).

Sanatan Dharma cannot be confined to specific rituals. It is a way of life that aligns with nature's laws. At its core, it emphasizes harmony with the planet. For instance, walking and moving defy gravity to some extent, yet humans are designed to walk, travel, and engage in physical activities. Such activities are categorized as *karma*.

People often ask what kind of work or actions they should undertake to lead a proper life. Scriptures provide a list of *karma*—actions to do and to avoid. These guidelines are not restrictive but aim to align human activities with nature. For example, living in high-rise buildings goes against the natural order to some extent.

Human life begins in the mother's womb, and the span of life is shaped by the experiences and nourishment the fetus receives. Therefore, great care should be taken during pregnancy, as the imprints formed then last a lifetime. Whatever stage of life one is in—whether it is *Brahmacharya* (student life), *Grihastha* (household life), *Vanaprastha* (retired life), or *Sannyasa* (renunciation)—respect for nature's laws is essential. Even in this conversation, where English is mixed with other languages, the emphasis remains on living according to the Dharma of planet Earth. It is a universal principle that applies to all aspects of life. We deliberately incorporated this concept. Our Hindi language is a remarkable achievement. However, when you speak in English, Dr. Jyotsna, can you recite the English alphabets? Can you say ABCD with us? The purpose here is to focus on the vibrations inside your mouth when you speak. These vibrations travel to the mind, and one needs to observe them carefully. Let us try: A, B, C, D, E, F, G. If you forget, you can say G. H, I, J, K, L, M, N, O, P, Q, R, S, T, U, V, W, X, Y, Z.

Did you notice, as you pronounce the letters, the upper jaw—particularly the gum near the first tooth on the right side—vibrates? This vibration impacts the left side of your body, gradually inclining it toward the right. This phenomenon can even lead to paralysis. That is the main cause of paralysis, Dr. Jyotsna.

Now, let us move to the Hindi alphabets, specifically the vowels (*Swar*). There are 12 vowels in Hindi, corresponding to the 12 zodiac signs that the Sun traverses annually. This connection is symbolic, as the Sun is a source of *Rajoguna*—an essential quality for action.

"What is your zodiac sign?"

"It's Libra!"

The Sun's movement across the zodiac imbues everything with *Rajoguna*. What is *Rajoguna*? It is a dynamic quality that enables all positive/negative activities. For instance, conversations like this require *Rajoguna*. Even adventurous or physically demanding tasks depend on it. Without *Rajoguna*, neither good deeds nor challenging activities are possible. These vowels in Hindi, along with consonants, reflect this *Rajoguna*.

Now, let us discuss the consonants: *Ka, Kha, Ga, Gha, Cha, Chha.* Pronounce them with me. When you say *Ka, Kha, Ga, Gha*, the center of your tongue strikes the upper jaw. This action generates vibrations within the body that enhance your immune system. Similarly, when you say *Cha, Chha*, your tongue lightly strikes your front teeth. Even the sounds *Pa, Pha, Ba, Bha* cause vibrations in your lips.

These vibrations have a profound impact on your overall well-being. Some people come to us feeling frustrated. I advise them to wake up early and engage in simple practices like chanting or using a calendar of Hindi alphabets . After a week, they report back, calling it a miracle. But it's not a miracle; it is the natural science and wisdom of our Rishis.

Our sages never took credit for their work. For example, we attribute many texts to Sage Vyasa, but who was Vyasa? His identity was not the focus; it was the knowledge he shared. Similarly, this wisdom is universal, beyond any individual's contributions.

Human beings, with their unique physique, are blessed. For example, as a neurosurgeon or neuroscientist, you might appreciate the profound alignment between ancient texts like the *Patanjali Yoga Sutras* and modern science. The *Yoga Sutras* consist of 196 aphorisms divided into four chapters: *Samadhi Paad*, *Sadhan Paad*, *Vibhuti Paad*, and *Kaivalya Paad*.

These 196 sutras align with the 196 nodes in the human body identified by modern neuroscience. Maharishi Yogi, who established an ashram in California, emphasized this correlation in his publications. It is remarkable how ancient wisdom and modern science converge, offering us tools to better understand the body and mind. Not everything is random; devotion brings particular vibrations or node within us. For example, when you feel anger, that too aligns with a specific node. These nodes govern the entire functioning of the body, including digestion. Ancient wisdom, like that of Patanjali Rishi, reflects a deep understanding of these processes.

Patanjali was not just a sage but also a kind of neurosurgeon of his time. The language of his era, Sanskrit, often referred to as *Dev Lipi* (the script of the gods), placed great emphasis on precision. All ancient scriptures were written for the welfare of humanity. What kind of welfare? To understand and align with the laws of nature.

The body is made up of various instruments (*yantras*), and our functioning depends on these instruments. Adi Shankaracharya, in his *Saundarya Lahari*—a hymn dedicated to the Divine Mother—describes these 100 instruments in detail. These instruments, governed by specific nodes, manage bodily functions. If an organ, such as the digestive system or heart, malfunctions, it means that particular *yantra* is not functioning properly.

This is why Indian sages emphasized *yantra sadhana* (worship of instruments), *mantra sadhana* (chanting of mantras), and *tantra sadhana* (understanding the physics of the body). The body itself is a *tantra* (a system), and the *yantras* within this *tantra* are interconnected. The mind, too, is a part of this system, influenced by specific letters like *y, r, l, v, sh, sh, sh, ha*. These nine letters shape the way the mind behaves.

The Rishis made extraordinary contributions by explaining how to live on Earth while respecting natural laws. For instance, humans walk on two legs, so they must follow the law of gravity. Animals, who walks on four legs, are less prone to sickness because their posture aligns better with nature.

A practical example is crawling. Babies crawl when they are physically at their healthiest, and even Shri Krishna is often depicted crawling while stealing butter. Crawling is a simple remedy for maintaining health. If you spend 5–7 minutes crawling in the morning, you activate blood circulation in the brain and keep your body's nodes functioning properly.

Even seniors or people with arthritis can benefit. By tying support around their stomach and knee can do crawling, they can enhance their blood circulation and feel energetic throughout the day. This practice ensures the proper functioning of all bodily nodes.

This was just a brief introduction. We can discuss specific diseases, like diabetes or arthritis, in more detail later. If you have more questions, we can continue with this topic or move on to something else, as per your preference.

Dr. Jyotsna Singh: " Swami ji You must return to discuss more topics on our platform."

Swami Ji:

If you enjoy something, you should carefully choose the language you use. As *Manishies* mentioned, focusing on certain aspects can be beneficial. Personally, I often speak in English, but I also use Hindi, depending on the activity. For example, while traveling by plane or engaging in short activities, English is convenient.

In today's era, nothing can be stopped completely. However, we must remain conscious of the larger impact of our actions. For instance, if we were to engage in a war or use nuclear weapons, we would need to consider the harm to the ozone layer.

We previously discussed *Yantra Shastra* (the science of instruments) and maintaining fitness. Let's take the Swastika as an example. The Swastika, which appears on the German flag, originates from Indian traditions and symbolizes the eight Vasus (deities). Our scriptures mention 33 gods, including 12 Adityas (associated with the Sun), 11 Rudras, and eight Vasus, along with Indra and Prajapati. The term "Aditya" is synonymous with Surya (the Sun), a concept from the Aryan traditions of North India.

In the Mahabharata, Bhishma, son of King Shantanu and Ganga, is identified as one of the eight Vasus. His story is well-known, especially after the advent of television serials. Bhishma had to take human birth due to specific circumstances, but he retained his divine connection as one of the Vasus.

The Vasus are connected to the human body through its nine doors: two eyes, one mouth, two nostrils, two lower openings below the navel, and so on. These doors are protected by the Vasus. The Swastika symbolizes these openings. However, the back door of the body is not included in this system because scriptures associate it with the origin of negativity.

The Swastika on the German flag is tilted, not upright. This symbol, a *yantra*, became significant during Nazi Germany. When the people of Germany collectively sang their national anthem under this twisted Swastika, it distorted the energy of their body's doors. This imbalance contributed to their aggressive behavior and, eventually, the Second World War. Such misuse of *yantras* highlights the consequences of misunderstanding their significance.

Even today, the effects persist. People in Germany face health issues and pandemics like COVID-19 or bird flu. This arises from how human energy interacts with others. In astrology, this interaction is called *Argala*, a concept from *Durga Saptashati*. *Argala* signifies the influence of one person's physical and spiritual energy on another, which can be both positive and negative.

On a larger scale, advanced technology in foreign countries creates issues like the destruction of the ozone layer due to massive bombs. Meanwhile, in India, spiritual traditions persist. A child growing up in a Western society may inherit a technological mindset from the parent, such as a software engineer. In contrast, an Indian child may grow up visiting sadhus and temples, finding joy in spiritual practices like ringing bells at a shrine.

This connection to spirituality is why Indian children are seen as devoted to Saraswati, the goddess of wisdom. India is neither excessively poor nor excessively rich but retains its unique spiritual wealth.

For example, let us consider the flag of Israel, where two intersecting triangles create a union. This union, similar to the concept of *Shiva-Shakti* in Sanskrit, represents a balance of energies. This is a profound idea, even amidst ongoing conflicts. The union of Shiva and Shakti has been elaborately described in *Triangle Yantra Shastra*. Now, if you take the example of a flag—keeping it upright and singing the national anthem for hundreds of years—such practices can draw people from all around toward this union of energies.

However, this focus on union seems to disregard the natural laws. As a result, negative impacts arise, leading to conflicts like the wars currently happening in surrounding regions. This lack of alignment with nature is one of the main causes of such unrest. *Yantra Sadhana* (worship or practice of instruments) has been explained, but the negative consequences of misusing it are not widely understood.

For example, if people listen to discussions on this channel or similar platforms, they may gain insights. My followers, wherever they are, might resonate with the idea. It is not about insulting anyone, but if changes were made—even as small as altering flags—perhaps these wars could be reduced on a large scale. We could then save this planet for humanity. Otherwise, we simply say *Hari Om* and leave the rest to unfold as it will, while others like Joshna Ji continue further on their paths.

Dr. Jyotsna Singh:

That's very good, Swami Ji. Let me introduce myself and the others here. Smita Ma'am and Vivek Sir are already present. Now, I would like to ask you one more question before inviting Smita Ma'am to speak.

Swami Ji, let's discuss the concept of time zones. Human life is often governed by desires, yet people fail to understand the essence of these desires. How can we achieve our desires effectively? What rules should we follow? Just as you spoke about the law of nature earlier, how can we align our desires with the concept of time zones?

Swami Ji:

Is this background song disturbing you at the moment? It's 5:30 here. I mentioned earlier that you might not be fully focused on listening.

Now, when discussing time zones, we can talk about latitude, longitude, or the broader concepts related to social dynamics. At the same time, we are also touching upon spiritual concepts.

Dr. Jyotsna Singh:

Yes, Swami Ji. Desires are a part of life. Even within spiritual practices, people have desires. The question is whether we can strike a balance. Can we integrate practical spirituality with a desire-driven life? How can we align both aspects so that they coexist harmoniously?

Swami Ji:

Of course, of course. First, let us understand the concept of time zones. I am speaking about something *beyond* time zones, <u>which is</u> the topic of our discussion today. Time, in Sanskrit, is called *Kaal*. In Hindi, we also refer to it as time, but *beyond* time is referred to as *Kaalateet* in Sanskrit, meaning "beyond time." This state beyond time is referred to as the *Mahakaal* state, a timeless state.

In the *Shrimad Bhagavad Gita*, Lord Krishna told Arjuna, "I am beyond qualities, beyond time, yet I value karma." This state of being beyond time is the *Mahakaal* state.

Now, time, as humans understand it, is a construct for convenience. For instance, the 24-hour time zone we follow completes one day. However, if you observe other planets, time differs. On Saturn, time spans a longer phase; on Jupiter, some longer; but on Venus and

Mercury, time moves faster, completing its rotation and revolution around the Sun more quickly.

When we talk about being beyond this time zone, we recognize how rivers, such as the Narmada River, are symbols of time in our scriptures. This is also a simple and relatable analogy. The cow is another symbol of time because it does not walk backward; it always moves forward. The same is said of the snake, which moves only forward. Both are considered worthy of worship—hence, we celebrate *Nag Panchami* to honor snakes and *Govats Baras* before Diwali, which celebrates snake and cow. These symbolize time.

When you cross a river, flowing in forward direction, symbolically, you are crossing time. Even if you cross a flyover with no river below but a forest or something else, unknowingly you flyover the snake or the cow, the act remains symbolic of crossing time. Such transitions represent entering a *Mahakaal* state—a state so vast and profound that it becomes challenging to control or fully understand.

Many people come to us here who have no direct connection to spirituality. Yet, they experience overwhelming influences, and we wonder whether these are the impressions of their previous lives. Were they some kind of spiritual teachers (*Babas*) before? Their karmic "paper" is vast, so we must address them accordingly.

In this *Mahakaal* state, people often justify themselves, proving they are "right." Desires play a significant role in this. The *Upanishads* mention three primary desires: the desire for a son (*Putraishana*), wealth (*Vittaishana*), and recognition (*Lokeshana*). Yet, in reality, there are countless desires—100, as per *Gautama Rishi's* teachings. For example, Indra, the king of gods, is said to have 100 pleasures, earning him the title of the king of enjoyment.

Desires, however, can become overwhelming. When desires intensify, they give rise to anger, which can also become uncontrollable. This manifests as "might is right." The crossing of a river, symbolically, reflects the escalation of such desires and emotions.

People often focus only on specific desires, such as sexual desire for progeny after marriage, but overlook the other 99 desires. These desires, combined, create an enormous weight, much like constructing massive dams. People do not realize how excessive their pursuits have become.

Take, for instance, modern lifestyles. Many individuals have wardrobes filled with clothes, countless pairs of shoes for different occasions—jogging shoes, bathroom slippers, and so on. People work so hard to acquire all this.

Evening comes, and instead of completing their daily routines peacefully, they continue pursuing unnecessary things, not knowing where to stop or how much is enough. Organizations like yours work hard to raise awareness, which is commendable, but still, most people fail to understand.

For example, when Morari Bapu recited 850 verses of the *Ramcharitmanas*, how many truly understood the essence of it? The grandeur was remarkable, and it must have been a deeply fulfilling experience for those present, but how much of its wisdom was internalized?

Why doesn't it affect the ascetics? Because when you accept a life of sanyasi or sage or sadhu so called, it symbolizes performing your own *shraddha* karma. The ritual of *shraddha* is performed at the *Brahma Randhra* (the crown of the head). This method is very profound.

As I mentioned earlier, either join the military and serve the nation or propagate religion, one person in kutumb (joint family) should do it and this was practice in ancient India which gives moksha to 7 generations, as scriptures says. Every individual is rushing just because of mahakaal state. These paths are acceptable for ascetics. I won't elaborate further, but desires keep escalating, and situations worsen.

However, consider the mental state—it's shaking. Look at the children being born today. Their rhythm is affected by mental activities, often taking unconventional forms. For example, actions that involve mental interference and tampering lead to significant consequences. Humanity itself is undergoing transformations. Faces are changing every day, and people are increasingly disconnected. Someone recently claimed to be possessed by a ghost. But it's not a ghost—it's the disorientation caused by being outside the time zone. People don't realize they are mentally and emotionally unstable.

This instability is observed in married individuals as well. Neuroscientists and neurosurgeons should note that this mental activity disrupts the natural rhythm. It's not about physical acts but about mental interference. From birth, humans are connected to their family members through bonds. These connections are established at a subtle level, starting with the mother, and extend through the navel to siblings and beyond.

If a lady has children, those children are also connected to her navel and siblings too are interconnected. These connections continue across generations. Such subtle connections influence even small children, who suffer because of these disruptions. Mental indulgence affects not just the mind but also the body, leading to illnesses such as sickle cell disease, brain tumors, and even breast cancer in women.

When the body's mechanisms break down, it results in severe consequences. The body has its natural mechanism, illuminated by the soul, which is its source, much like the Sun is a source for Earth. Without the soul, the body loses its vitality. In spiritual terms, the soul is Shiva. Without the soul, the body becomes an empty vessel. Even if the immune system is intact, the absence of the soul renders the body non-functional.

When mental activities interfere, the body's system—its *yantra*—begins to break. If this *yantra* breaks, it creates an imbalance. This concept connects to the Pingala, Ida, and Sushumna nadis (energy channels). If one end of a *yantra* is connected to another's body, it begins to draw light from the other's soul. This sharing of light can create a temporary sense of strength and joy, but it also leads to darkness and imbalance.

When parts of our *yantra* break or shift, it affects not only us but also those around us. For example, if an instrument within us tilts or breaks, it becomes a burden on our relatives. Our physical and mental disorientation impacts our connections. Photons—energy particles—move between bodies, further complicating the process.

When an electron gives space in ones body, the photon enters another. This transfer affects the body's balance and creates disturbances in the energy systems of relatives. Often, we remain unaware of these subtle dynamics. These imbalances are significant and have far-reaching effects on the physical and spiritual planes.

So, when someone in your family, a blood relative, falls ill, the doctor does an analysis. The doctor says this person does not have symptoms of diabetes. Diabetes has many symptoms, such as eyesight weakness. This means there are many symptoms. A homeopathic doctor closely analyzes it, and nowadays, modern science also does many experiments. So, the doctor says that these are the symptoms, but it is not possible that this person has diabetes. Still, there is suspense. Well, who is making this person sick? There is nothing bad in your family member.

Now, this decline in nature, the other person is not doing anything, yet what is happening? How is he getting so much strength? I do a lot of activities. Who is nourishing him? Who is making the other person sick? Well, is it a disease? It is only named that way; all those diseases are being suppressed. Now, look at the direction in which society is moving. In this time zone, only by crossing this river, can you achieve it. In yoga, you can go, and you can achieve a state of timelessness. There is a return from that. In yogasana and pranayama, there is a very beautiful kriya called yoga nidra. If you practice yoga nidra, then during that time, your entry into all parts of your physical life is possible. You lie down in shavasana, and there is a return. No one touches your body, and no movement occurs. This return is a game of beyond time.

Now, you understand anger.

Dr. Jyotsna Singh: Swami ji, you have explained it very nicely. There is another guest among us, Sunita mam, who also wants to say something.

Swami ji: So, I had asked her to join. Hari Om!

Smita Potnis: Hari Om, be happy. I want to ask. I would like to ask that you have mentioned timelessness and genetics. Can you tell us what a timeless thought is?

Swami ji: We are not clear about your question.

Smita Potnis: Timeless thought. You have told us about genetics, but what can be a timeless thought? You can tell us about it in terms of spirituality as well as science.

Swami ji: Of course, of course. Timeless thought is just imagination. But there is a lot of spiritual imagination in it. Your soul is located at the navel, in the center. From any level, measure the height of the body above it. It is the same as the height from the navel to the feet. That means we are talking about the Shikha (the top of the head). The part of the body above the navel is the same length as the part below the navel. The space between them is where the light of the soul is handled.

Your whole bladder, the tummy, contains the liver and the thalamus at the head and its tail, for males, we have testicles for that purpose. Now, from where are you thinking? From the navel, from your thalamus, and below the navel. If your thought process is below the navel, then this is imagination.

In the timeless state, this imagination is very vast. If you are imagining in anger, you will attack the person in front of you with all kinds of scenarios, like the ones shown in cartoon films. As for desires, you may be served all kinds of dishes on a golden plate. These kinds of imaginations have been mentioned in stories. In texts imagination are said Mahisha (black), Mahisha means black, and to kill these imaginations, there is a form of Durga called Mahishasur Mardini , who is the demon-slayer. Now, there is a very good story in this. This has also been told by the sages. You must have read the story of Vishwamitra Rishi. A king came to him, and Vishwamitra vowed to send him to heaven while he was still alive. The king was later called Trishanku because Indra refused, and he was suspended somewhere in between. So Vishwamitra Rishi, who was not a Brahmin but a Kshatriya, became a Raj Rishi. The glory of a Raj Rishi and a king is such that whatever they say, how can there be a Rishi against that? When Vishwamitra became a Raj Rishi, Indra said, "O Lord Rishi! He is ALIVE If you send him, it will not be acceptable because this is a subtle state." If you want to send him, you should create your own creation. Create a heaven for him. This story illustrates this point. Send him there. Then Vishwamitra Rishi said, "Of course, I can do it." He said, "You can certainly do it. Who would take enmity with the sages?" Even Indra defended himself. He said, "But I have a suggestion for you, Rishi. You should first make a cow, like the Kamdhenu cow. You will get convenience and help too." So Rishi liked this idea, and when he went to make a cow, it turned out black. The buffalo you see is the cow made by Vishwamitra Rishi. The imagination as story says is black. So, this is a subtle, timeless state. I will now talk about another subtle system.

Parashuram ji, who was a sage, is one of the only sages in North India who has crossed Narmada river to enter deccan state. Now, let's see how beautiful this geographical creation of ours is. It is said that *yat pinde tat brahmande* (as is the body, so is the universe). You can understand all these things very easily. If you look at the night sky toward the north, you can see the Sapta Rishis. There are seven stars called the Sapta Rishi. Their names are given in our Puranas: Vishwamitra, Jamadagni, Bharadwaj, Gautam, Atri, Vashishtha, and Kashyap Rishi. These gotra (lineage) started from them. In the south, Agastya Rishi's name is very popular. Now, Vishwamitra is the son of Jamadagni Rishi. Sorry, I was talking about Parashuram. Parashuram Rishi belongs to the lineage of Kush. Parshuram Rishi, the son of Jamadagni Rishi, crossed the Narmada River, and after crossing it, he entered the timeless state. After entering this timeless state, he killed 21 times Kshatriyas with his axe. Anger does not stopped till Ram avtar. You see, a person experiences two types of youth. First, he is going to fulfill his desire, knowingly or unknowingly even interacting with the woman who is in distant and height of anger as said. You spoke of the subtle state, discharge of sperms in PARA state, and then you see the three dots on the coconut. You can refer pic of sperm with 3 dots and tail in coating. This is proof of Parshuram Rishi's actions. Rishiputra Parshuram tells that he crossed the river. If you look at the book on coconut cultivation in the school library, or elsewhere may be library of Thanjavur, you will learn that coconut cultivation began only after Parshuram crossed the river. Though *Krishi Shastra* is written by *Bhardwaj Rishi.* This transformation of Parshuram happened at a subtle level. You can say this was the work of the sages of the lineage they have left examples or in other words alarm that The activity is not favouring law of planet earth. For example, when we discuss the work of Sage Patanjali, Dr. Jyotsna has asked a good question. Sage Patanjali was a great neurosurgeon, just like Sage Sushruta was a surgeon. Sage Patanjali was a neurologist, and Sage Sushruta a surgeon. He created his own surgical instruments, or you can call them tools, which had blades for surgeries such as caesareans. All these instruments had a fish tail shape. If you hold that fish tail, like during a caesarean, then at a subtle level, Rajoguna (one of the three gunas or qualities) increases in you, and you start shaking. Understand what I am saying and do not take it in any other way. If you are a married surgeon, whether from India or abroad, the law of planet earth are the same everywhere. This is the definition of DHARMA—the law of universal nature. So, if surgery is done correctly with these instruments, and if you are married, that is good. If a tailor holds it, that is good as well, because without it, the tailor cannot shape the cloth properly. The gardener or barber will also hold it. This was the example given by Shankaracharya when he was declared Jagadguru at Kanchi Peetham in the ninth century, after he became Digvijaya (victorious over the world). He defeated everyone in debates and re-established Sanatan Dharma, the law of nature. Then, after everyone declared him Jagadguru, a barber came forward. He said, "Jagadguru Shankar, you will only be the Jagadguru if you can answer my question." So, Shankaracharya asked him to tell his question. The barber said, "I am a barber, and I want to know how to shave." Shankaracharya said, "Sit down, and I will tell you." So, he applied soap, and as soon as the barber sat down, Shankaracharya held the surgical instrument, the razor. One of his fingers, little finger, stood up, and when he went to shave, he said, "No, I have come to know that our cleaner repeatedly says that anyone who holds this type of knife with a fish tail becomes mentally engaged, and this is why mental engagement happens. The reason is that Rajoguna increases inside you." You are not doing anything, just holding that particular knife, and that moment is not the same, but it is a good example, like the buffalo. This example of Parshuram Rishi has been taken in a different way by people today, but there is intelligence in it. Without that moment, it is not possible, I am saying, sizering delivery . Surgery is not possible. I don't know why this topic came up, but it is related to surgery, so this is the reason. Imagination becomes so vast, it is imagination. And to get rid of it, Mahishasuramardini, the praise of Durga, is needed. Everything about the law of nature, how to cure this type of demon, and when you go to temples and worship Durga, you start receiving the same type of cure. You imagine this and that should be done in a certain way. What is the science you are talking about?

Smita Potnis: No, I have thought about the timeless...

Swami Ji: The timeless state, a zone beyond time, is the state of Mahakaal. Everything is Vast, your thought process and prayer, you don't know where to stop. The means of return you feel is to fulfill desires, you get caught in your physical existence, but not in your true place. Otherwise, you find satisfaction in anger and fulfilling your desires, and this is its result. The scriptures say that the local river of the village where you were born is your deity. It will fulfill your desires. The local Bhairav and goddesses do the work of procreation for you. The goddesses protect you. But crossing this, you must be conscious, even at a subtle level, and you can notice this practically.

Smita Potnis: Thank you.

Dr. Jyotsna Singh: Thank you so much, Smita ma'am, for asking such a beautiful question. We have all learned from it. And thank you, Swami Ji, for taking out so much precious time to come to our platform and sharing all these insights so beautifully, giving us such a good message. Smita ma'am, before you leave, please give us a message if there's anything you haven't understood yet.

Smita Potnis: The timeless thoughts that Swami Ji mentioned, I feel that whatever we imagine is connected to each other. If we grasp something from others, we get something in return as well. So, everyone is connected to each other, and the imagination that is unified from there is probably timeless. This is how I understood it.

Dr. Jyotsna Singh: Thank you, Swami Ji, for also taking your precious time. We must maintain the dignity of time, so the discussion is going very beautifully. But the dignity of time...

Swami Ji: So, he should practice it at least once a day. This is a message to all of you: thank you all, and I am happy. But once he learns the Hindi alphabet, he will get some relief from the human system and its problems. Later, we will understand the law of nature. Okay. Hari Om.

Dr. Jyotsna Singh: Hari Om, Swami Ji. Many tha*nks*

QUESTIONNAIRE ON DIABETES

Dr. Jyotsna Singh: We are live. Hello everyone, and welcome once again. Today, we will be having a very important discussion about a topic that affects at least one person in almost every household: diabetes. We will delve deeply into understanding what diabetes is, why it occurs, and how it develops.

Our guest today is a renowned scholar who has conducted extensive research and brings a unique perspective to this subject. The insights shared today will be crucial, so it is important for everyone to listen to the entire conversation. Diabetes is now a widespread condition, affecting people in nearly every home. Alarmingly, it is no longer limited to adults but is increasingly seen in children. I have come across many cases where diabetes has been diagnosed at birth, as well as in children as young as 6 or 9 years old.

We will explore what steps can be taken to manage and control diabetes effectively. Is it something that lies within our control? What changes can we make in our lives to address this condition? To help us understand this better, I welcome Swami Ji, who has previously graced this platform with his enlightening talks. Today, he will share his wisdom about diabetes in a truly distinctive manner.

Please pay close attention to his advice and try to implement it in your lives. The experts who join us on this platform dedicate their valuable time to share their knowledge, and their guidance has the potential to transform lives. This platform exists to make such life-changing information accessible to all.

Feel free to ask your questions during the session. Thank you very much, and I now hand over to Swami Ji to share his insights on how we can address and manage diabetes. Over to you, Swami Ji.

Swami Ji: Diabetes! First of all, *Hari Om* to everyone. Diabetes, in itself, is not technically a disease. It has been clearly explained in the scriptures by the sages. The cure for diabetes is connected to the worship of Saraswati. The Saraswati you know—commonly invoked with verses like *Kundendu Tusharhardhavala*—is often recited in schools and early education settings. Saraswati is regarded as the mistress of all *rasas* (essences).

What are these *rasas*? In our body, the *sapta dhatus* (seven essential elements) are referred to as the seven *rasas*. Saraswati governs them. When these *sapta dhatus* start depleting or wearing out, the body experiences a deficiency in sugar, which is referred to as diabetes. So, diabetes essentially arises due to a lack or depletion of something in your body.

When diabetes is diagnosed, the first treatment is usually insulin. Along with that, you may be given glucose or sugar. But the sugar that your body produces with insulin is derived from only one *rasa*—out of the seven on which life is sustained. These *sapta dhatus* form a sequential chain in the body: first comes *rasa* (the essence derived from food), which forms *rakta* (blood), from blood comes *mamsa* (flesh), from flesh comes *majja* (marrow), from marrow comes *meda* (fat), from fat comes *shukra* (reproductive essence or semen), and finally, *ojas* (vital life energy) is formed.

When these begin to deteriorate, sugar levels in the body decrease. The glands, especially the pancreas, fail to produce the necessary juices or perform their functions properly. As a result, physical symptoms emerge—weak eyesight, difficulty sleeping, memory issues, frequent urination, constant fatigue, and an overall lack of vitality.

Your diet plays a crucial role here. Often, it is said that you rely on just one *dhatu* for sustenance. Many restrictions are imposed on you, and sugar seems to be present in almost everything. Even the food you consume contains glucose, which is essential for forming the body's juices. Fruits and other foods contribute as well.

When diabetes occurs, it may feel like life has become limited or depleted. However, this can be reactivated—

if you worship Saraswati. According to the sages, certain temples play a significant role in this healing process. For example, there is a connection with Shivalayas (Shiva temples). In one of my earlier talks, I mentioned Kedareshwar and Bhim Nath. Bhim, during the Dwapara Yuga, established a Shiva Lingam on the southern bank of the Narmada River. This region was once ruled by a demoness named Hidimba, and her son Ghatotkach was born to Bhima. Worshiping the Shiva Lingam here, known as Rasheshwar Mahadev, can help restore the strength of the *sapta dhatus*, thereby addressing diabetes.

So, if your question is why diabetes occurs, it essentially stems from the decay or depletion of the *sapta dhatus*. Are you following this?

Smita Potnis: Maybe it's a network issue. If we are talking about worship, then how is worship done?

Swami Ji: You are worshiping Saraswati everywhere. Saraswati is the source of creation. As mentioned in the scriptures, even Brahma Ji has said that Saraswati played a role in aiding his creation. If you look at the composition of the *Panch Mahabhut* (five elements)— *Aakash tatva* (ether), *Agni* (fire), *Vayu* (air), *Jal tatva* (water), and *Prithvi tatva* (earth)—the earth element itself is created from water. Whether it is the formation of a child in the womb or the creation of any compound, water plays a crucial role. For instance, this planet Earth is also said to have been formed from water. The sages described Earth as *Anasuya*, the daughter of Kardam Rishi. By the way, *Datta Jayanti* is approaching, and Kardam Rishi, as per his name, is associated with mud or soil—*kardam* means mud.

Now, you may find this surprising. Are you from Maharashtra? From Mumbai?

Smita Potnis: Yes, yes.

Swami Ji: In Maharashtra, there is a very famous *Ram Raksha Stotra*. It was composed by *Budh Kaushik Rishi*. *Budh Kaushik* translates to "owl." The scriptures describe Earth as the daughter of Kardam Rishi. This planet's physical form is created from water—whether it's a drop of water or any other compound, the process is similar for other planets. Even the Sun, in its compound form, contains the water element.

The growth or development of this water element is referred to as Saraswati. This development of *rasa* (essence) is the process by which solid food in your body is converted into *rasa*, and from this *rasa*, your entire body is formed. So, if you go to any Shiva temple and worship Saraswati—through whatever means you know, whether it's a *rasa* (essence), a mantra, or even if you don't know any mantra—then you are connecting with Saraswati.

In South India, there is a specific form of worship dedicated to *Raseshwar Mahadev*. Do you know what mercury is? Those who achieve mastery (*siddhi*) over mercury prevent the *sapta dhatus* from decaying. In many districts of the South, if you worship *Raseshwar Mahadev* or Saraswati at a Shivling in any Shiva temple, it helps in preserving the *sapta dhatus*. The process is straightforward.

Smita Potnis: Yes, my question was that if there is worship, there must be some chanting of mantras. Chanting has an effect on the body. For example, insulin is given externally to control glucose. Does chanting mantras have any impact on this?

Swami Ji: See, insulin is essentially a life-saving drug, but it does not strengthen your *sapta dhatus* (seven essential elements) or activate your pancreas. Instead, it deactivates the pancreas. This organ is responsible for generating sugar in your body, and insulin does not help it function—it simply provides an external dose of sugar regulation.

Now, some people have genetic defects even before birth. What role do their parents' conditions play in this? We have observed many such cases where defects in the water element occur. Mantra worship is recommended to help the mind focus. When the mind is disturbed or worried, chanting mantras is prescribed. You cannot give just any mantra to anyone—specific mantras are meant to address specific concerns. Mantras help focus the mind on a particular task, which is why a mantra for a particular deity, like Saraswati, is given.

For Saraswati worship, it is very simple. The mantras taught in school, such as *Kundendu Tusharhardhavala* or *Shubha Vastra Vrata*, can be used. You do not need to be overly serious about mantras. Ayurveda also offers remedies to activate the pancreas and restore the *sapta dhatus*. For example, there is a well-known Ayurveda laboratory in Hyderabad. An Australian missionary, back in 1917 and later in 1997, worked with Ayurvedic scholars across India to create effective formulas and opened a laboratory called Dishen Company (J & J Dishen). They produce a capsule called *Mersina*, which is highly affordable—only ₹1 per capsule. It is designed to activate the pancreas and help restore the body's *sapta dhatus*: *rasa* (essence), *rakta* (blood), *mamsa* (flesh), *majja* (marrow), *meda* (fat), *shukra* (reproductive essence), and finally, *ojas* (vital energy).

In contrast, insulin simply works directly, without guiding the body in a specific direction. When the *sapta dhatus* are in balance, they resonate with the seven colors (like VIBGYOR) and seven musical notes (*Sa Re Ga Ma Pa Dha Ni*). When diabetes occurs, this harmony is disrupted. Have you seen goddesses in iconography holding sugarcane in their hands? For instance, Goddess Lalita holds sugarcane, symbolizing the importance of sugar in life. In our traditions, offerings like jaggery and water are common—sugar mixed in sherbet is consumed, especially in the summer, to restore energy.

Diabetes occurs because Saraswati, the flow of water and essence in the body, is disrupted. When your body's processes slow down and stop converting food into further energy or essence, this stagnation leads to long-term deficiencies. Worshiping Saraswati or *Raseshwar Mahadev* at a *Shivalaya* (Shiva temple) can help. Worship here simply means bowing down, showing reverence, and acknowledging the deity as your source of light. Even if you do not know a mantra, simple chants like *Om Namah Shivaya* or *Namo Raseshwaraye* are enough. Bowing down at the Shivling strengthens the body's essence.

Mantra worship is not overly complex. For example, you can simply say, *Saraswati Deviyah Namah* (I bow down to Goddess Saraswati). Performing *jalabhishek* (offering water) or milk offerings at a *Shivalaya* works too. The *Shivalaya* is a symbol of creation, and there is a reason why every village in India has one. The concept of the *Shivling* reflects a deeper understanding of creation and the universe.

Science, as we commonly know it, is referred to as "a-para" (material knowledge)—that which is not spiritual.

But the *Shivling* symbolizes *para gyan* (spiritual knowledge). The spiritual and material worlds are interconnected, as expressed in the phrase *yat pinde tat brahmande*—whatever exists in the body also reflects the structure of the universe. Just as there are countless galaxies, there is a similar reflection of that vastness within your body.

Swami Ji: If you are born on Earth, then the sand particles here have been analyzed even by modern science. It has been said that by studying these sand particles, you can estimate the number of stars in the galaxy. Similarly, from this *pindi* (a representation of the universe, like the Shivling), you can estimate the number of suns. This knowledge has been shared in a concise form. Just as this *pindi* is created from water, the stagnation of water—its lack of movement—leads us to analyze why such stagnation occurs. For instance, why does diabetes happen?

The literature available in medical science is focused on the material aspects of the world. It does not explore the process of reactivating the pancreas or producing essential bodily elements like the *sapta dhatus*. Instead, the responsibility of management is handed over to the individual. However, the *para jagat* (spiritual world) explains through the concept of the Shivling that your thoughts are directly connected to the effects of your actions, like performing *jalabhishek* (offering water) on a Shivling. Since the body is primarily made of water, the thoughts in your mind generate vibrations within your water molecules. When you pour water on the Shivling with certain thoughts or intentions, those thoughts are amplified and take shape.

The Shivling represents the origin of creation, and your thoughts play a crucial role in shaping outcomes. If many people visit a Shivling with the same thought or intention, the collective energy manifests in that direction. In Maharashtra, the Lingayat community has a practice of placing a Shivling on the *samadhi* (memorial) after cremation. These memorials radiate waves linked to the intentions of the person who has passed—whether it is winning a court case, arranging a marriage, or freeing a field. This concept shows the profound nature of the Shivling.

In spiritual practice, chanting mantras charges the water molecules in your body. Similarly, prayers for procreation or health can have an impact without requiring a visit to a temple or the chanting of specific mantras. The feelings and intentions in your heart initiate the process, helping your *sapta dhatus* regenerate. When this happens, conditions like diabetes can improve, as it is closely linked to the functioning of the *sapta dhatus*. For example, sugar, which is essential for life, is often restricted for diabetic patients in modern medicine. However, Ayurveda advises diabetic individuals to drink sugarcane juice regularly, as it helps restore the balance of *sapta dhatus*.

Now, addressing the cause of diabetes—it is not truly a disease but rather a lack of presence of mind. After marriage, a unique hormonal exchange occurs between the husband and wife. The X chromosome of the female interacts with the X chromosome of the male, and vice versa. This exchange changes the composition of their bodies. The male body has both X and Y chromosomes, while the female body has XX chromosomes. After marriage, the husband's Y chromosome aligns with the right side of the wife's body, and the wife's X chromosome aligns with the left side of the husband's body. Y chromosome of man governs the thought of females

When the couple is separated for even a short period, they begin to miss each other, and this hormonal interaction starts to impact their bodies. During this phase, the *sapta dhatus* begin to decay. The thought of the partner who has contributed to the body's composition leads to mental engagement, which can contribute to physical decay. For example, women may develop tumors, particularly in the lower back region, on either the right or left side. Men, on the other hand, may develop sickle cell issues or experience other signs of decay in the *sapta dhatus*.

This decay manifests as exhaustion, excessive thirst, and a desire for water or sugary drinks like *sharbat* to restore energy. Symptoms include blurred vision, knee pain, and blood clotting. The decay of *sapta dhatus* is an indicator of deeper mental and physical interactions.

Even among smokers, a similar phenomenon occurs. A smoker may feel comfortable alone but feels the urge to smoke when another smoker appears. Similarly, newly married couples often think intensely about each other, leading to these physiological effects. Women with tumors in the back or spine often display signs of this process. There are numerous examples of families facing similar challenges. This morning, an elderly man came with his two daughters-in-law, sharing a story that reflects an ongoing pattern. It is important to consider how these issues affect their children. Spirituality tells us, and the sages have also said, that until the age of four, a child reflects the conditions and problems of their mother.

For instance, a case came to us involving a child around three to four years old. The child had already undergone three operations for kidney stones and was carrying a urine bag with a pipe attached. When asked about the situation, the family explained that despite three surgeries, no stone was found. I observed that the child, being so young, could not have naturally developed stones. Instead, I advised the mother to get herself checked. Upon examination, it was revealed that the mother was the one with stones, not the child. Despite the child undergoing repeated operations, the problem lay with the mother.

Similarly, between the ages of 5 and 8, a child starts reflecting the conditions of their father, regardless of whether the child is male or female. For example, some girls perform poorly in their studies. In such cases, instead of focusing solely on the child, the father needs to undergo treatment. Families often fail to recognize this interconnectedness.

From the age of 9 to 12, scriptures state that a child begins to reflect on their ancestors and the unfinished tasks of their lineage. They intuitively inherit the duty to complete these tasks or carry forward the family's responsibilities. In Sanatan Dharma, this is symbolized through the *Janeu Sanskar* (sacred thread ceremony). The three strands of the thread signify three debts: the debt to the motherland, the gods, and the sages.

However, "gods" here do not mean divine figures alone; the first god is one's mother, who gave birth. Similarly, "sages" do not exclusively refer to ascetics with long beards; they represent our ancestors and their wisdom. Lastly, the motherland, the place of birth, holds a debt to be repaid. Whether born in India, Nepal, China, or elsewhere, one carries this obligation.

A case highlights this principle: a woman with a tumor had a two-year-old child who could neither speak nor walk. I advised her to treat her tumor and have her husband tested for sickle cell anemia. Many do not realize that children reflect the conditions of their parents, including unresolved issues like these. Often, conditions like diabetes remain hidden for years because they are linked to underlying issues like sickle cell anemia.

Such problems arise from the depletion of *sapta dhatus* (seven essential bodily tissues), which occurs due to mental interactions with one's partner. Modern medicine does not address these deeper connections. For instance, diabetes is not truly a disease but a lack of knowledge. If sugar is completely avoided, the body cannot generate energy. Energy production requires sugar, making its restriction counterproductive. Diabetes is, therefore, a consequence of ignorance rather than a medical condition.

Dr. Jyotsna Singh: Absolutely correct. I would like to interrupt here. It is absolutely true that diabetes develops in our body over time, often without us realizing it. It can remain undetected for years. When symptoms finally appear, it is often part of a chain reaction, where diabetes can lead to or accompany other diseases. At this point, I would like to ask Smita ma'am if she has any questions about what Guruji has shared so far. Please, go ahead.

Smita Potnis: I actually have already asked a question. However, there is something I read that I wanted to bring up. It was in the *Bhagavad Gita*. It mentioned remedies for diabetes that involve achieving peace of mind through spirituality. From what I understood, it suggested that spirituality can help manage or even transform the diabetes within us. I don't remember all the details, but maybe you can clarify this?

Dr. Jyotsna Singh: Let me explain this scientifically. Diabetes, like any other disease, begins to take root in our lives based on our daily habits and emotions. The foundation of many diseases lies in our feelings, particularly negative emotions that we carry inside us.

For example, we may get hurt easily over minor issues or experience excessive anger. Anger, in particular, is a significant factor. But it's important to know when and where to express anger. Awareness of our emotions is crucial. Jealousy is another common negative emotion—for instance, when someone else achieves success or wealth, many people feel jealous instead of content.

Other emotions like irritation and frustration also contribute. These can be triggered by the smallest of things, like a laptop not working or difficulty with a phone. Some people let such small frustrations dominate their entire day, creating a cycle of negativity.

Now, here's the good news: all these negative emotions can be removed. There are various techniques, tools, and methods available to help us release them. The moment you make a conscious effort to let go of these emotions, your health will begin to improve, and you'll start living a healthier, longer life.

If we look at our ancestors, many of them lived up to 90 or 100 years of age. Why? Because they didn't approach life with a sense of relentless competition. Today, people are constantly running after money, chasing it endlessly, yet often finding no real satisfaction or results at the end of the day.

The key takeaway here is not to stop striving for a better life but to stop letting material pursuits dominate your peace of mind. The balance lies in focusing on emotional and spiritual well-being as much as physical health.

Swami Ji: Someone once asked me, "Do you want knowledge or money?" I replied, "Everyone is giving knowledge—just send money!" This frustration you feel, look at creation itself for an answer. For example, right now, we're experiencing a technical fault where our voice is echoing back to us. It's frustrating because we can't fully understand the problem, and as a result, we're speaking loudly. But this is a small thing compared to the broader creation around us. Let us explore how things are created and what we might be missing.

Take something as simple as salt. In the past, if salt was kept outside a house, even thieves wouldn't steal it. Salt creates distance—it signifies separation. Giving someone salt can signal a breakup in a relationship, while giving sugar, like in the form of sweets such as *ladoos* or *pedas*, indicates goodwill and connection. All celebrations involve sweets, not salt. This reflects the subtle messages in creation.

Diabetes is connected to the *Sapta Dhatus* (seven elements). Its remedy is Saraswati worship. It's simple—you don't even need mantras. Just visiting a Shiva temple with a pot of water in hand and offering it to the Shiva Lingam, with pure thoughts, can initiate creation and balance within yourself. This act symbolizes consecration, and through it, your body and mind begin the process of healing.

Ayurveda offers straightforward solutions, including medicines that stimulate the pancreas. If insulin is required, it should be used only for a minimal period because diabetes itself is not a disease. Instead, it is a result of imbalance. The lack of sugar in the body can lead to many other ailments, as sugar is essential for energy and functioning.

Understanding the *Sapta Dhatus* is key. Creation begins with water; our origins are rooted in water. This is why we have the concept of the *Panchayatan*—the five principal deities of Indian spirituality: Shiva, Parvati, Ganesh, Vishnu, and Surya. All other deities are considered extensions of these five. In this system, every act of creation can be traced back to water.

When a child forms in the mother's womb, profound changes occur. The child originates from water and juices in the mother's body. Bones are formed from water, blood from juices, flesh from blood, and so on, until the entire structure, including the glow on the skin, reflects the health of the individual.

Many women experience symptoms like vomiting, frequent urination, or skin infections during pregnancy. These changes are due to the additional energy and creation happening within their bodies. Post-marriage, individuals often degrade their *dhaatu* (essence) through mental strain and interaction, which ultimately depletes their *Sapta Dhatus*. This lack of balance can lead to diabetes or other issues.

Now, why does frustration occur? It's because things don't go as the mind desires. Even children feel pressure from their parents, who unconsciously pass on their mental and physical imbalances to their offspring. This cycle of interaction affects the child deeply.

In Indian traditions, mothers shape their child's early values (*sanskaras*) up to the age of four. After this, the father takes over and performs the *Yagyopaveet Sanskar* (sacred thread ceremony). The child is then sent to a *Gurukul* for formal education. Historically, sages didn't even lift their children into their laps until they turned four, as it was believed this stage belonged solely to the mother.

But today, children get caught in the emotional and physical imbalances of their parents. Parents themselves carry unresolved issues like tumors in the mother or sickle cell in the father, which often have roots in the health and habits of previous generations.

Understanding these principles of creation, balance, and heritage helps address issues like diabetes—not as a disease, but as a reflection of our deeper connections and imbalances.

Swami Ji: Someone asked me, "Which would you prefer: knowledge or money?" I replied, "Everyone is giving knowledge—just send me the money!" This is a lighthearted way to address frustrations, but let's delve into the deeper issues of creation and balance.

Take the example of a child in the mother's womb. The mental and physical state of the mother directly interacts with the child, influencing the development of the *Sapta Dhatus* (seven elements). This interaction, even during pregnancy, can cause a natural decay in these elements, creating pressure on the child. The process of creation within the womb involves continuous churning—similar to how the Earth rotates and revolves. This churning shapes everything, from fingerprints to the inherent nature of the child.

The *Sapta Dhatus* are formed through this process, starting from water. The chromosomes (*XY* for males) play a role in determining what is built. In Sanskrit, the mother's womb is referred to as *Kshetra* (field), and the father contributes the *Seed*. This aligns with the concept of *Kshetra Kshetragya Palini*, a name in the *Lalita Sahasranama*, which describes the nurturing power of the divine feminine. The goddess Lalita is connected to this act of creation.

This knowledge, as found in the Vedas, is often misunderstood. For instance, *Sanatan Dharma* (eternal law) is not a religion but a universal law of nature. If one aligns their life with these principles, they remain healthy and balanced. The *Lalita Sahasranama* was imparted by Lord Hayagriva, a divine figure with a horse's head, to Sage Agastya. Horses, being highly attuned to nature, symbolize the subtle connection with the Earth's energies. The *Samaveda* is associated with horses, *Atharvaveda* with monkeys, *Yajurveda* with goats, and *Rigveda* with cows. Each Veda reflects lessons drawn from these creatures' interactions with the Earth.

Creation begins with water. In the womb, the body develops step by step: fluids become blood, blood becomes flesh, flesh forms bones, bones gain marrow, and eventually, the glow of health appears. The *Sapta Dhatus* form, but the mental and physical states of the parents can introduce imbalances. The soul itself is formed from the eighth essence or *rasa*. This process resembles the churning of curd into buttermilk, with the soul emerging like butter rising to the top. The soul, too, is a kind of essence or juice.

The child's mental state is also affected by the mother's emotions and interactions during pregnancy. Parents' unresolved issues, whether physical (like genetic conditions) or mental, can manifest in the child. In traditional Indian culture, mothers instill values (*sanskaras*) in their children up to the age of four, after which fathers guide them until they are ready for formal education in a *Gurukul*.

Returning to creation, the soul gives energy and vitality (*Yogbal*). Without the soul, the body cannot function. The mind, however, is dualistic and acts as both a support and a challenge. The mind introduces poison (negativity), but creation depends on this duality—without negativity, positivity cannot exist. Just as the churning of the ocean produced both nectar and poison, creation is born from this balance.

Even artificial methods of creation, like test-tube babies, cannot replicate the natural blessing of the womb. This divine process involves a higher level of complexity and balance. Each aspect of creation, from the *Sapta Dhatus* to the soul and mind, reflects the interplay of natural and divine forces.

This discussion of creation, rooted in ancient wisdom, underscores how every step—whether in the womb or in life—is influenced by subtle energies, interactions, and dualities. These principles remind us of the sacredness of natural processes and the importance of maintaining balance in body, mind, and soul.

Swami Ji: Let's complete the discussion on creation and numerology. The process of creation, from one to nine, is a continuous cycle. The essence, which is the ninth element, represents the mind, and the mind has both a positive and dark side. Both sides have power, as they emerge from the process of churning. Just like Earth, which has both trees that bear fruit and thorns, creation encompasses both aspects. People often say they want to live in the jungle and renounce the world, but even in such a life, difficulties arise. For example, when doing the *Parikrama* of the Narmada River, the thorns you encounter represent the hardships of creation.

The numerology of creation, starting from one, progresses through various stages. For instance, one plus one equals two, and when subtracting one from two, we get zero. This zero is known as space in the cosmic context (*Bramh Bramh*), and creation in this space is explained simply. Originating from water, and the seven metals are formed. These metals decay due to the mental attraction or influence. The eighth metal, however, represents the soul and willpower.

This is the transition period, and the upcoming *Navratri* is significant in this context. Just as in the previous *Mahishasura Mardini* story, this *Navdurga* journey—from *Shailputri* to *Mahagauri*—is about removing the negativity in the mind, as creation is rooted in the mind. The Brahm, the space, the churning, all these processes illustrate how diabetes is not a central concern. What matters is how willpower and the strength of the soul can help overcome such challenges.

Even if you don't go to a Shiva temple, creating a small clay Shiva Linga at home can be a form of healing. Perform daily rituals, such as anointing it with water. Some people even make Shiva Lingas from mercury, which is purified and used in a specific way, but your thoughts and intentions are what matter. The Shiva Linga is a symbol of birth. When a man and woman meet, it is auspicious, symbolizing the birth of something new. The cure for diabetes is simple, and Ayurveda provides valuable insights for longevity.

The Rigveda, which speaks about cows, teaches us much about life. Ayurveda similarly teaches us through nature, such as the Shami tree, which is considered the queen of plants, and the Shwetark tree, which is regarded as the king of plants. If you pray to these plants in the right manner, they can offer wisdom. Just as we received the Rigveda from cows, Ayurveda offers knowledge about healing through nature.

I am running out of time, so we will continue this discussion later.

Dr. Jyotsna Singh: Thank you so much, everyone. I apologize for having to wrap up the program due to time constraints, but we will hear more from Guruji next time. He explained beautifully about diabetes and its origins. Thank you, Smita Madam, for coming here, and thank you, Guruji, for your wonderful insights. Thank you, everyone.

Swami Ji: Best of luck with your next lecture.

REWIRING OF MIND

Dr. Jyotsna Singh: Hello everyone! Along with today's good evening, I want to share how delighted I feel as we delve into programming our minds. Our guest today, a distinguished individual with immense knowledge and experience, needs no lengthy introduction—I can summarize their expertise in just two words: deeply insightful. They have dedicated significant time to studying these topics.

Today, we will discuss how to program our mind, body, and soul. Revitalizing these aspects is not a simple task; it's profound. How can we integrate scientific understanding with spiritual practices to achieve this? Why is it important, and what steps can we take? This discussion is especially relevant to the youth who aspire to achieve so much but often feel stuck. Success, fame, and recognition are deeply desired in today's world, and many find themselves comparing their lives to others.

Recently, someone came to me, distressed by the success and fame others seemed to achieve effortlessly. They kept asking, "How do they have so much money? How have they reached such heights?" After listening, I suggested they focus on reprogramming their mind instead of being consumed by comparison. Everyone's journey is shaped by their struggles and efforts. The key is to introspect and understand our own strengths and path.

Today, we have Swami Chaitanya Ji with us, who will shed light on this subject. I urge you to listen closely, especially if you feel disheartened or unsuccessful. He will provide detailed insights on how to rewire our mind, body, and soul to unlock our potential and achieve success. Swami Ji, please guide us, particularly for the younger generation facing these challenges. Over to you, Swami Ji—please elaborate on this important topic.

Swami Ji: Hari Om to all! Thank you, Dr. Jyotsna, for including the younger generation in this initiative. Guiding young people ensures their growth, and they, in turn, can guide their children. This is why so much emphasis is placed on educating the youth. Sanyasis like Swami Vivekananda focused on youth. Today's youth often trust Google more than their Gurus. They search Google for answers to everything. However, the knowledge of Gurus is encapsulated in *sutras*, which are concise and profound. Unfortunately, those who interpret this knowledge, including creators of platforms like Google, might not fully understand it. Moreover, today's youth are too preoccupied with earning a livelihood to delve deeply into these teachings.

Our effort is to convey this wisdom not in complex Vedic language, *Shrutis*, or *Richas*, but in simple, everyday language. We aim to connect youth with knowledge about the mind, body, and soul. You mentioned how to shift the mind from negativity to positivity, which is excellent. But first, let us understand how all of this originates and functions within the body. If we start with the mind, we observe that every action begins with a thought. Regardless of whether a person weighs 50–60 kg or stands five feet tall, a thought arises in the subtle mind. This thought drives the body to act—whether it is planning a pilgrimage, studying, or simply craving *golgappas*.

But what exactly is the mind? Even surgeons cannot pinpoint its exact location within the body. This invisible mind systematically moves the body and initiates actions. If we wish to cultivate the human being, we must first understand how humans were formed and why negative thoughts like jealousy arise.

It is said in simple terms that the food we consume shapes our mind. Food becomes juice, then blood, and ultimately forms our entire physical compound. In our previous discussion on diabetes, we explained the journey of food through the *Sapta Dhatus*—blood, flesh, marrow, fat, semen, and energy. For example, when you eat fruit, the juice within the fruit contributes to this process. Similarly, grains like rice, wheat, and lentils also contain water. Crops grow through water, and this water element manifests in our body as juice. This juice transforms into blood, flesh, and bones, ultimately producing *ojas* (vital energy) and soul.

The soul, like butter from churned curd, is pure and floats above the impurities. It acts as a catalyst in the body, enabling all functions and activities. Just as the sun catalyzes crop growth on earth, the soul sustains the body. Interestingly, while the soul is derived from the water element, poison is also created from water. The mind, being opposite to the soul, represents negativity and poison. Despite being opposite, it possesses immense power.

Take Maheshwar, for example, a small town on the northern bank of the Narmada River. Here, we find numerous goddess idols with demons or devils beneath their feet. Similarly, Shankar Ji's Dakshinamurthy form also depicts a demon lying underfoot. These demons symbolize the mind—poisonous and opposite to the soul, yet powerful. Understanding this opposition helps us comprehend the mind's nature and its role in our spiritual journey. The soul is described as *Amrit* (nectar of immortality). It is positioned above the arrangement of the seven metals in the body. If we talk about the letters in the body, as we previously discussed regarding the *Beyond Time Zone*—beyond time and space—we learned how vowels and consonants are formed.

There is *Rajoguna* (a quality of passion and activity) within me, which derives its strength from the Sun. The 12 vowels are formed due to the Sun's movement across the 12 zodiac signs. In each letter, for instance, if we say "Ka," *Rajoguna* is present. Even in "Ka," the pronunciation ends with "A." Letters like "Ka," "Cha," "Ta," all have *Rajoguna*. The nine letters "Ya Ra La

Va," and "Sha, Sha, Sa, Ha" represent aspects of the mind. These letters signify the nine forms of negativity within the body.

The letters "Ya Ra La Va" are purely poison, entirely opposite to the soul, and hence opposite to *Amrit*. They are formed within the body, and this formation relies on water, which the body obtains from food and its juice. The journey of the *Sapta Dhatus* (seven bodily tissues) begins with juice and culminates in the eighth element, *Amrit Makhan* (nectar-like butter), which exists in the body as a catalyst for all functions. However, the mind, opposite to this nectar, also arises. The mind, equally powerful as the soul, manifests in nine forms of negativity. These correspond to the nine aspects of the world. Thus, before reaching the soul, one must also address the mind.

To deal with this, the concept of *Navadha Bhakti* (nine forms of devotion) is introduced. Numerology also points towards the mind, from numbers one to nine. All of this takes place within a single space: the ovum in the mother's womb, where creation occurs. The ovum, or egg, is central to all forms of life. Just as a dove, rooster, or hen originates from an oval-shaped egg, humans also originate from an ovum.

When the sperm from the semen enters the ovum, the juice of the body enters this oval-shaped egg. This illustrates that the body is composed of water. The food one consumes and the thoughts one harbors charge this process. The water molecules in the body, influenced by mental waves, become charged. As mentioned earlier, water in a glass or pitcher in a household reflects the dominant thoughts and ideology of the household.

When a guest drinks this water, they can discern the nature of the household's ideology. Similarly, the sperm that enters the ovum carries the charge of thoughts and food consumed by the individual. The ovum is referred to as *Brahmm*—an empty canvas where creation takes place using water and sperm which is referred as *Brammha in texts*. From this one element, the entire body is formed. The mind, with its negative tendencies, must retire within this space, and positive action must arise from it.

To cultivate this, ancient systems recommended attending a *Gurukul* in a state of celibacy. Today, people go to school, but the principle remains—what kind of thoughts are nurtured, and what kind of literature is studied, plays a crucial role.

By the age of four, a child is prepared to enter an educational institution, starting their journey of learning at five. Over time, the water element in their body develops. In the modern era, this process often continues until a person is 20, 22, or even 25 years old, after which they enter married life. Through marriage, they create a child like themselves. The thoughts, food, and waves that shaped the parent are transmitted, and the child's mind is influenced by the wavy water inherited from the father. In which *Gurukul* or school, and up to what level, was the father educated that influenced the water element in his body? You know this as a fact: men's bodies consist of 70% water element, while women's bodies have 77% water. This water element, inherited from the father, plays a critical role in the formation of a child. This concept has roots in the Upanishads and Vedas.

The "one ear" of the father resides in the mother's womb during pregnancy. The child, in the womb, retains *Shruti*—what is heard and remembered. But whose *Shruti* is this? It belongs to the mother. The child hears their mother's voice, which becomes ingrained as *Shruti* in their memory. When the child is in the womb, the water element of the father forms their body. The womb, the mother's house, becomes the place where the child hears these *Shrutis*.

The mother interprets the water element and communicates it to the child through *Shruti*. In the Vedas, *Shruti* refers to sound, and hymns represent the vision or waves of the father's water element. Only one "ear" of the father contributes to the creation of the child, while the rest dissipates. The child develops within the womb, nourished by the particles around the ovum and protein intake. This process embodies the concepts of *Shruti* (heard knowledge) and *Smriti* (remembered knowledge).

The child absorbs these *Shrutis* and hymns while in the womb, and once born, retains them as memory. These retained *Shrutis* guide the child's life. This explains the formation of the mind. If a person's mind becomes disturbed, there is a simple way to correct it.

Swami Ji: Hari Om! We have understood this up to here. Let us proceed further, shall we?

Dr. Jyotsna Singh: I want to add to this. You mentioned that when someone drinks water from a place, they can adopt the thoughts and energies of that place. This resonates with my own experiences. For instance, people often invite me to deliver lectures or consult patients. On one occasion, I drank water at a particular place and immediately felt uneasy. Something strange overtook me. Later, I asked them if there were frequent arguments or significant problems occurring in their home. They confirmed that such issues were common. This made me realize that water absorbs and reflects the thoughts and energies of those around it.

Swami Ji: I'd like to expand on your point, Dr. Jyotsna. You'll find this interesting. As a doctor, you meet many patients daily, and you encounter numerous situations. Today, we live in a time when much of this happens even on platforms like Facebook. If someone tells us something there, we don't always process it deeply, yet we are affected.

All humans and creatures are composed of the water element. Let me share an observation. Have you ever noticed how the water element connects to every face? Look at the face of any creature—even a lizard. Have you ever closely observed a lizard?

Dr. Jyotsna Singh: Yes!

Swami Ji: Look at the lizard. It walks on walls, yet its face is distinct. Similarly, the face of a human is unique, as is the face of a cow or any other creature. The face is always forward-facing, while the rest of the body follows, much like a tail. If you observe the sperm, its shape mirrors this structure—it is like an arrow with a distinct head and tail. This morning, we found a small arrow. It reminded me of this concept. When split, the sperm reveals three dots, similar to the three dots on a coconut. This connects to the mythology of Parshuram Ji, whose iconography features a peak resembling the structure of a sperm. Peel away the outer layers, and you'll notice that its shape is akin to the growth of forests and life itself.

Water itself is inherently wavy. Its molecules vibrate with energy, which is why rivers hold such spiritual importance. Festivals like Diwali encourage bathing in sacred rivers like the Ganga, Narmada, Kaveri, or others because they carry the energy of continuous chanting of divine names, such as Harinam. This wavy, sacred water is believed to cleanse sins, reflecting its vibrational purity.

For a man to contribute to the creation of a child, his body, composed of 70% water, must be groomed and purified. This body cannot be formed by blood, flesh, marrow, or fat alone but relies on the essence of semen, specifically the sperm within it. To generate high-quality sperm, a man must practice celibacy for up to 25 years, as per traditional wisdom, ensuring his vitality. Similarly, the egg of a woman must resonate with the same purity and energy to nourish the developing child. Pregnant women are therefore kept in peaceful environments to groom the baby correctly.

In such households, you'll often find continuous efforts to maintain a harmonious atmosphere. The children born into these environments inherit these vibrations, carrying the *Shruti* (knowledge heard) from their time in the womb. This ingrained memory shapes their personalities, making them uncomfortable with anything that goes against this *Shruti*.

Dr. Jyotsna Singh: This is true. As a doctor, I encounter many patients and environments. Sometimes, I drink water at a place and feel uneasy. It's as if the water absorbs the conflicts or energies of that house.

Once, I asked a family if they often argued or faced many problems at home. They confirmed it, proving that water reflects and stores the energy around it.

Swami Ji: Exactly. This phenomenon underscores how the water element, present in all living beings, connects to our thoughts and actions. Consider this: every human face, much like the structure of the sperm, reflects this connection.

For example, the *Surya Siddhant* explores the minutiae of time and cosmic order, dividing a single second into 3,750 parts. This granularity emphasizes how deeply nature's laws govern us. Through such texts, we learn that water molecules can be charged with our thoughts. This is why mantras are so important—they charge the water within us, influencing our mind and body.

However, mantras must be approached with care. Some universal mantras, like *Om Namah Shivaya* or *Om Namo Bhagavate Vasudevaya*, can be chanted without initiation. These resonate with universal energy. But other mantras require proper guidance from a Guru. Mispronunciations or improper recitation can negate their effects.

For instance, the correct pronunciation of Krishna is not "Krishna," but *KRUSHNN*. Such nuances matter because vibrations influence the energy of the mantra.

Many people chant without understanding these subtleties, leading to inefficacy.

To address negative thoughts, begin by focusing on positive energy. Place a glass of water before you and imbue it with your positive intentions. This charged water can help purify your thoughts and align your mind. However, it's essential to judge whether your positive thinking benefits others and does not stem from jealousy or selfishness.

In essence, the mind, powerful as it is, requires deliberate grooming through positive acts and charged intentions. Only then can we navigate the challenges of life with clarity and peace. If we begin thinking from that perspective, we realize that there is no separate concept beyond this—it aligns with the eternal principles of *Sanatan Dharma* and the laws of nature. These laws inherently govern everything, including our thought processes, which also fall within their domain. Let's proceed with this understanding.

Dr. Jyotsna Singh: As Swami Ji mentioned, the key is to focus on the intention behind your thoughts. It's crucial to understand that your mind doesn't differentiate between positive and negative thoughts in terms of value—it simply responds to your feelings and emotions. So, if you're thinking negatively, the mind doesn't understand what is good or bad; it only reacts to how intensely you're focused on those thoughts. This is why it's important to consciously frame your thoughts in a positive direction.

Swami Ji: Now, let's talk about the thought process. As you know, women have 77% water in their bodies, which is more than men's 70%. Science confirms this, and this higher water content can make women more susceptible to emotional impacts. For example, if there is any negativity in a woman's water element, the effects can be quite powerful. Take Ahilyabai Holkar, a warrior who defeated many opponents and built temples all over the world. She came from a small family in Aurangabad, but her history reveals the incredible strength of women. When we discuss how to keep women positive, the focus is on maintaining balance in their emotional state.

In Sanatan Dharma, there are practices related to the care of one's hair. Women traditionally tie their hair up to avoid the negativity of open hair, as it is said to reflect their emotional state. If a woman's thoughts are positive, her water element will also be positive, but if they are negative, the results can be damaging. Men also have similar practices, such as wearing a turban or keeping a Shikha, as a way to maintain balance and avoid negativity.

The ancient sages, like Agastya Rishi, knew the significance of managing the water element in the body. According to the story, Agastya Rishi drank ocean to control the water element. He also taught that tying the hair helps manage the negative energy and emotions in a woman's body, allowing her to overcome difficulties.

In this context, our thoughts must follow a pattern—thought, silence, thought, silence. This rhythm allows for a balanced flow of energy and mental clarity. The mind and thoughts drive both the body and the soul, functioning as catalysts. A discussion we had with a person during Shivratri revealed that the Vedas describe water molecules—hydrogen and oxygen—as being connected to the Rishis Mitra and Varun, symbolizing the fundamental building blocks of life. The story is presented like this: the interpreter misunderstood it. He was not from India but from Germany. He wrote that two sages, Mitra and Varun, were watching the dance of an Apsara (celestial dancer) in heaven, and they ejaculated, causing rain. He said this is written in the Vedas, referring to the phrase "Varun Tvam Vishtam," meaning water. However, the real message is about the Apsara, who serves as a catalyst. The word "Apsara" comes from "Aap," meaning water, and water is referred to by many names in Sanskrit. One such name is "Aap," and those who roam in it are called Apsaras. This is related to water, and the discussion leads to the idea of rain.

Now, where do hydrogen and oxygen come from? It is said that when the 300th layer of the sun explodes, waves emerge. This layer contains oxygen, and the 27th layer contains hydrogen. When they combine in the Earth's hemisphere, it leads to rain. This narrative reflects how the story of water shapes our thoughts. It's important to understand the thought process here.

For example, as a doctor, a baby in the mother's womb is not doing anything else but forming from a single water molecule, which we call sperm. The sages have safeguarded this process for 25 years to understand the laws of the Earth. It's not just about rituals but about daily discipline, including how we sleep, wake up, sit, walk, and earn money. These instructions, followed with care, charge your "water" with that one drop of life. This was the sages' thought process.

Later, the creator in the womb takes that drop of sperm, and the egg inside it is also called Brahm, representing creation in an empty space. Within Brahm, this drop of water silently creates life. The thoughts start here—first, to build up your own water molecules, and then, as a child, to have the same potential and capability. So, creation happens in a silent, empty space, one drop of water at a time.

The process of thought and silence works together. After completing a task, like finishing a conversation, you enter silence. This is when you charge a glass of water with positive thoughts, and then drink it. You can also charge your food with positive thoughts. That's why people take precautions before eating in hotels, or after receiving alms, where water is sprinkled with mantras like the Annapurna mantra. Although I do not know the exact mantra, the idea is to fill the water with positive thoughts. By doing so, you charge your food, which you then consume. This positively affects your body, forming the blood and nourishing the bone marrow.

This process is key. When you eat food, with positive thoughts charged into it, your body silently absorbs that positivity. Thoughts stored in your body, particularly in the water (which makes up 70% of the body), guide you. A person who does this will never be defeated. Their actions will always be guided in the right direction, avoiding any wrongdoings. This is the way to understand and grow the mind.

Dr. Jyotsna Singh: This is a wonderful thought, and I am sure our viewers are understanding how, by combining science and spirituality, we can see the importance of water. Water is essential for life. Without water, we cannot even eat once. Water is extremely necessary for life, and it plays a very important role. Every human being has it, right? So, if you drink water after charging it with positive thoughts, you must focus on positive thoughts. Say to yourself, "Everything is going well in my life." If you repeat this once, twice, or even three times, within a week, you will start to notice improvements in your life. I can see that if you start practicing this, you will see how much better your life will become. Just do it. And before we conclude, Swami Ji, please share a positive message for the younger generation so they can practice and apply this in their lives. Please give a message before we finish.

Swami Ji: For the youth, karma should never be neglected; karma is essential. Lord Krishna has always said to Arjuna, "I love karma." However, while performing karma, it is important to think about yourself. These days, you need to think about yourself. But you must also consider the process of food. Whatever work you do to earn money, save for the future, raise your children, groom yourself, and take care of your family, you must keep in mind whether what you consume is helping build your physical body. Whether it's food or drink, you should ask yourself: is it made with positive thoughts? Not just water, but everything you consume. If it is not made with positive thoughts, you should transform it by filling it with your own positive thoughts through positive conversation. After that, you interact with it, because your body is made of water, and the water molecules in your body can be charged. If you want everything in your life to be positive, you need to build yourself in that way. It is your personal life. To achieve this, you may need to fast or pray with positive thoughts for five minutes with your food in front of you. You may need to talk positively about it. By doing so, you will build your physique. You are the one who creates it, and you have only one medium to build your body—through food and water. Whether it's tea, coffee, milk, juice, buttermilk, lassi, or just simple roti and sabzi, everything you consume creates juice in your body, which is essentially creating water. If you fill it with positive thoughts, it will be positive. Many young people today eat food from hotels—pizza, burgers, and so on. They may not realize the importance of changing their mindset toward food.

In today's fast-moving world, let it continue. There is healthy competition, yes, earn money, save for the future, and build your future. But whatever you consume, if it is not made with your own positive thoughts or prepared by your mother or wife at home, you should still charge it with your positive thoughts. Then, you will see how everything turns positive. No negative thoughts will enter your mind. I have shared the key idea: the mind is made from water. This is a crucial point, and that was my message.

Dr. Jyotsna Singh: Thank you so much, that was beautifully explained. This understanding of the mind's wiring and how it relates to the body and soul is something you can apply universally. The formula that Swami Ji shared today is a life-changing approach. If you follow this for even a month, I am confident you will progress by 10 years. This is the way to grow in life. Through this platform, we hope to change many lives. So, I want to thank Anil Sir and Swami Ji for giving their precious time and being on this platform. I also want to express my gratitude to our team, who are doing such a great job.

Swami Ji: I appreciate them. Yes, they are doing excellent work. Their communication is great; they always make sure everything is right before going public. This is my third appearance here, and I'm grateful to all of you. I've noticed the personal problems you address, and how you interact with many. I've seen how you've interviewed scientists and various professionals. You all are well-established in your respective fields. Keep up the good work. We will also charge the water with positive thoughts, and you should go forward. And your team, too. Good, keep it up!

Dr. Jyotsna Singh: We need your blessings to continue our work.

Swami Ji: We can only guide you, and in simple terms, remember your body is made of water, and water is essential for the future too. This has been going on since the beginning of time. So, keep it simple—take five minutes before drinking water, say positive thoughts, or recite a mantra if you have received Guru Diksha. Be happy, forget everything, and focus on those thoughts. Then, keep silence. When it's time to eat, take a few minutes to think positively, and then keep silent. That's the thought process. Hari Om, Om.

Dr. Jyotsna Singh: Thank you, thank you! Hari Om.

QUESTIONEIR ON VASTU : CHALLENGE OF THE DEMON

Nikita: GMWST, before we begin with this workshops, I would like to share a few words about a truly divine personality, Swami Ji. Swami Kalpataru Chaitanya Ji is a disciple of Paramhansa Swami Satyanand Saraswati Ji. Swami Ji received the teachings of Karma Yoga in 1977, which are renowned through the Ganga Darshan Ashram in Munger, Bihar, widely known as the Bihar School of Yoga.

Swami Ji has mastered various disciplines like Yoga, Pranayam, and more. Swami Ji's dadaguru Maharaj Ji, is Swami Shivanand Saraswati Ji of Rishikesh, associated with the Divine Life Society. Swami Ji has elaborated on concepts of the mind, body, and soul, including how the soul evolves, how one can metaphorically "cross the river" to enter the Mahakal state, and ways to combat diabetes through Shivalaya Sadhana. Swami Ji has conducted deep studies in all these areas, and his knowledge is a gift to all of us.

Today, we are blessed with an opportunity to hear from Swami Ji, who is not just an ordinary personality but a divine one. Currently, Swami Ji is in Nagpur for Chaturmas. Let us take this opportunity to gain insights for a peaceful and blissful life. Swami Ji, I request you to take over the platform. On behalf of everyone, I am truly grateful for this opportunity to listen to you. Please guide all participants. Hari Om.

Swami Ji: Hari Om, thank you very much. I would like to know if the participants are comfortable with Hindi for active listening and communication.

Nikita: Yes, Swami Ji. My request to all participants is to note that although most of them are from India, there may also be participants from other countries. However, Hindi is a language through which we can express and exchange our feelings effectively. Swami Ji will also use English as needed.

Additionally, if you have any questions during the session, please raise your hand to maintain decorum. Swami Ji will address all your queries during the Q&A session, which will follow his discourse. Let us now begin the session. Hold your breath and welcome Swami Ji. Sachin, over to you. Welcome, Swami Ji.

Swami Ji: Thank you once again, and my thanks to Khandelwal Ji. Today's topic is *Vastu Shastra*. When Mr. Vivek Bajpai proposed this topic, he gave it a very interesting title: *The Engineering Behind It*. However, I suggested changing the title to *Challenge of the Demon*. This is because *Vastu Shastra* falls under the domain of Mayasura, an Asura known for his expertise in architectural and structural construction. According to tradition, any concrete construction faces the challenge of Shankar Ji's curse.

At present, when we think of *Vastu Shastra,* it is often associated with structures such as houses, schools, colleges, hotels, government offices, and other buildings. However, beyond concrete construction, the essence of *Vastu* lies in a broader perspective.

If we look closely, the human body itself is an extraordinary example of *Vastu*. It is a beautiful creation and a form of divine engineering. This human body is formed in the womb of the mother, a process that many of you are familiar with. From the seed of a man, known as sperm, when it enters the ovum, a process of construction begins. In Hindu philosophy, this ovum is referred to as *Brahmm*. In our scriptures, *Brahmm* signifies an empty space—a blank canvas for creation. Contrary to common misconceptions, *Brahmm* does not signify something external; it represents the space in which creation occurs.

The sperm initiates creation in the *Brahmm,* forming a human body like ours. The same process applies to all species—for instance, in hens and roosters, the sperm and ovum together create life in a similar manner.

To understand *Vastu* fully, we must first examine our own body as an example. Each particle of sperm acts like a craftsman within the ovum (*Bramha*), shaping every part of the body: the eyes, nose, mouth, and other organs. In our scriptures, the creator of this process has been metaphorically referred to as Parashuram, who represents the craftsman or engineer of this divine construction.

The *Vastu* of the human body is deeply influenced by the Ashram system. Before marriage, in the *Brahmacharya Ashram,* a person follows a disciplined life, which prepares the body for the next stage of life, the *Grihastha Ashram* (marital stage). During this stage, the charged water molecules in the body (sperm) create new life, forming a human with unique mind and intellect.

The thoughts and waves within these water molecules shape the mind and intellect of the individual. This is where the connection to *Dashavatara* comes in. For example, Kalki is not merely a future avatar, but a metaphor for a complete human being formed in the mother's womb over 9 months and 9 days. Similarly, Parashuram represents the crafting process within the *Brahmm,* the divine canvas where creation takes place.

The human body also contains 10 "doors," which symbolize the sensory and functional pathways. Above the navel, there are seven doors associated with the mind. Below the navel, females have three doors, while males have two.

To truly understand *Vastu Shastra,* we must explore these aspects of the human body and mind. Only then can we move on to the concept of physical construction and its relation to the spiritual principles outlined by Mayasura and other ancient texts. One door is in front of the navel, and another is on the backside. It is said that the female physique has three doors, while the male physique also has three doors. The structure of the third door differs between males and females. In females, the 10th door is external, making them naturally extroverted and expressive. This is why it is often said that women do not "digest" things—they tend to express their emotions and thoughts outwardly.

In males, the 10th door is internal, which makes them introverted by nature. Men do not typically express themselves as freely as women. This internalization is why scriptures state that men are more suited for *tapasya* (penance). Whether it is spiritual rituals, hard work, or earning money, these efforts require a disciplined, introspective nature. For example, we are here in the studio of Sandeep Agarwal, a hardworking entrepreneur and engineer. He is so dedicated to his work that he has been on a liquid diet for one and a half years and continues to work tirelessly, even on Sundays. This dedication exemplifies the masculine trait of inner focus and effort.

This difference in construction between males and females also influences their mental and emotional behavior. Men often rely on the understanding of others rather than expressing themselves openly, while women express themselves more freely. The soul, which governs the body and mind, resides at the navel. As Khandelwal mentioned earlier, the soul plays a central role in how the body and mind function.

The *Vastu* (architecture) of the human body is constructed from water particles. The sperm forms every part of the body—the eyes, nose, mouth, and other features—through a process guided by *Parashuram,* the symbolic craftsman in Hindu scriptures. When the child is born and cries, that act is associated with *Rudra,* symbolizing the beginning of life.

This process of creation within the womb is not isolated; it is influenced by the rotation and revolution of the Earth. Just as the Earth rotates on its axis and revolves around the Sun, these cosmic movements impact the development of the human body. This connection is evident in fingerprints, which serve as proof of the Earth's laws being embedded in us. Similarly, the stripes on tree leaves reflect the Earth's rotation and revolution. This cosmic churning mirrors the creation of the human soul, much like how curd churns to produce butter.

The soul is created within the womb through this process of churning. The ovum acts as a blueprint, and the sperm replicates it to form a new life. The soul is akin to the essence that makes the body kinetic, enabling all functions. This principle applies not just to humans but also to the Earth itself. The Earth's rotation sustains life, and if it were to stop, the planet would die—just as the human body cannot function without the soul.

The scriptures state that the soul is located at the navel, which serves as the central point of the body. The light of the soul radiates from this point to energize all organs. If any part of the body receives less of this "soul light," diseases occur as dead cells accumulate in that area. This is why fasting is encouraged—it allows the soul's energy to distribute evenly throughout the body rather than being consumed by the digestion of heavy food.

In spiritual practices, saints and sages guide individuals to direct the light of their soul toward healing specific ailments. This soul light also illuminates the ten senses, encompassing the senses of knowledge and action. The body (*Pindi*) created by *Bramha* follows the same cosmic laws that govern the Earth.

Now, turning to concrete construction, these principles of *Vastu*—the balance of elements, the churning of energy, and cosmic influence—are foundational. The body, strengthened by seven metals, serves as a template for understanding the architecture of both physical structures and the soul. Before proceeding, I would like to request Miss Khandelwal to ask if anyone has any questions in between—Mr. Vajpayee, Ashok Ji, Mr. Sandeep Agarwal, Dr. Deepa, Dr. Chhabra, or anyone else. If you have any questions regarding the conversation so far, please feel free to ask.

Dr. S Chhabra: No, sir, thank you very much.

Swami Ji: Miss Khandelwal, has anyone raised their hand? Mr. Kapil, yes?

Kapil: I like to ask, first of all, Namaste sir, and it was great knowledge from you, thank you. Sir, my question is that there are many such alternative solutions like Vastu, Feng Shui, and Japanese and Chinese models. I would like if you can shed some light on this, I will know the difference a little bit. So, thank you, thank you.

Swami Ji: Thank you for your question, but we have not entered into concrete construction. Right now, we are talking about the physics. We are talking about physics. Do you have any doubts?

Kapil: No, it is all clear, sir. It was fantastic, thank you.

Palak: Sir, I have one question.

Swami Ji: Yes, Palak, please go ahead.

Palak: Sir, the soul is called immortal, then how will the soul be created? It already exists, right?

Swami Ji: Now, Palak, you're a student of which subject?

Palak: Sir, I am a student of biotech, but I am very active spiritually. In all these things.

Swami Ji: I am a biotech student! You tell me, from where is this planet Earth getting light?

Palak: From the Sun.

Swami Ji: Of course, no, if it is not the Sun, is it possible? So the Sun is mortal, and do we have light?

Palak: Maybe we can say it's mortal.

Swami Ji: After being a biotech student, you can be concerned with technology. So Palak, the thing is that, the Sun is also not immortal, but it is so bright, if your soul, like you are female, your soul is also like a water drop and its light is so bright like the Sun. Female, what happens, soul is placed in your understanding, right? And its shape is exactly like a water drop. It is narrow at the top and its bottom is a little broad. Instead of the shape of a diya, instead of the flame of the diya, there is such a place in females, and to handle the light of this soul, you have a tummy in which the bladder is present and a thalamus on the right and a point comes towards the thalamus of the female, it is upside down in the male. How is it upside down in the male? Its bottom is broad in the female, similarly in the male, the upper side is broad and its point is in towards the testicles, right, so it is upside down. What is the reason that when this split happened, you must have read the law of limits, when this split happened, then the male is having a tail and the female is receiving through the tail. That is what thing is split, right. Just like it was split. There is a difference in these two physiques, so it decides accordingly. So do not put more liability on females. Females are good company, good companions. Because the sunlight is going to a point in their thalamus, it is not so in males. In males, that light is going completely in the thalamus. Males compare as the sun, and females compare as the moon receiving something from males. And the solution to that light, every fight, every problem, is found only by females. Because it is fierce, there is so much light in the thalamus and it does not know sometimes. How to control? Then he finds the mother, their sister, their wife as the better half, and the right. So they find the solutions. Solutions. They think very slowly. Ultimate solution in that matter. No immortal concern, it is not concerned about. Soul you have a life. In human physique, every physique having a soul. Same to same is produced on earth. Otherwise not possible. At what distance? Do there is difference? The closer the planet is to the Sun, the more it resides, not above. The farther it is, the more foggy the weather is. There is smoke. Proper light, that is why the soul's place is in the navel of a human. Vastu, we are having a topic on. A good question.

Palak: Okay, sir, thank you.

Swami Ji: Okay, right. CSK, any question? Vivek? We will proceed. 23 others and also here. Mahesh Gupta Ji, okay fine. Okay, now we are jumping into the concrete construction site. So we understood a very big principle of construction that you have to do construction with the help of water and in construction also, exactly like you charge the water, after that you gave an offering there. Right. And as it is said in the scriptures that offer food to the *Bhhag*, the female vagina is called *Bhhag*, *Bhhag may Bhog say Prapti,* so if you offer food to the vagina, make sacrifices in it, like you perform yajna etc., then you will get fruit.

In the yajna kunda also, we have the shape of the vagina in which you offer the ghee and other offerings, and your wishes are fulfilled. Yajna is also called that which fulfills your wish. By offering certain things in the havan, you attain results from it, as described in the scriptures. Construction relates to anything that you want to build; you have to offer sacrifices, and to offer sacrifices, a man has sperm, by offering which, another human being is created. Now let us also know its limit. Let us move to the second phase. The scriptures say that if you offer sacrifices for progeny, then you will attain the desired result. Otherwise, in whichever vagina you are offering sacrifices, that vagina takes the offering. For example, look at the conch, it is moving a little fast, and this raises another question. We rarely see a conch, but its shape is similar to the vagina. It is always said to be kept immersed in water; otherwise, the conch will take its pleasure. So, the human body discharges automatically.

That is why it is said that seeing the vagina is a sin. Seeing the vagina causes sin, so whoever worships the yantra knows this. Worship the Shri Yantra, worship the Kuber Yantra, worship any yantra. It is forbidden to see the yantra. So, whenever the yantra is placed, it is placed at the chest level so that you can see it as a triangle-shaped yantra, and the triangle is like the wings of a butterfly. This is the triangle shape of the yantras, and seeing that part is said to be a defect, otherwise, your sacrifice is done. You ejaculate, whether it is sex, or a yantra, or any other thing, because there is no other way to reproduce. Right, now after saying this, when you go for concrete construction, Mayasura, about whom it has been told, is the enemy, the demons. There is a small background to this too. Mayasur, the demon is also father – n- law to Ravan. He has a boon from Shankar Ji that whoever does construction will have to sacrifice himself, and he will sacrifice, and lose everything. Mandodari is the name of Mayasura's daughter. So when you go to do concrete construction, at that time your semen ejaculates. And as soon as your semen ejaculates, it becomes something constructive, concrete, which is not physical (human physic). In this way, you keep giving your sacrifice every day after constructing a house, you are giving your sacrifice. Understand this in a simpler way: the importance of celibacy is mentioned in our scriptures. If you meet a female, and the second time is not committed, then after marriage, if you meet a female a second time, you sacrifice yourself. Why? Her soul is opposite, and she pulls it so quickly that you dump it there in the light of your soul. Everything.

Nikita: Sorry for the disturbance, Swami Ji, please mute yourself. Everyone, please keep yourself mute. Please proceed, Swami Ji.

Swami ji: Everyone is married, and here I am talking about this. This is the second time your intelligence has engaged with your better half. In another instance, you might have to sacrifice your body, and the female is devaluing you for your physical form. I didn't marry; I consider myself fortunate. I notice many women now expressing dissatisfaction with their husbands. They come to me and say, "Maharaj, what is your problem? Your husband isn't with you."

Today, with courage, I said, "What is the issue? If this topic keeps coming up, it's a good thing. I've

heard that husbands often don't get such opportunities. If this is being discussed, it's not bad. In fact, what could be worse than this? It's actually a good thing. Hey, tell me—leave external discussions aside and talk internally, talk inwardly. Isn't there a voice from within the body telling you what needs to be done, what needs to be placed where? You also notice this, and I don't know what we do, but others notice it too. They also listen, they also understand."

So, Maharaj, the question arises—are such people suited for the Sanyas Ashram? Have they left worldly attachments behind and given themselves back to us? This is true. Every woman after marriage hears the voice of her soul. She offers sacrifices according to the role or instrument (medium) she is aligned with. The male becomes the deciding factor. The concept of *Ardhanarishwar* (half-male, half-female form of Shiva) begins here. From the same sperm, whether a human baby is created or something lifeless is formed, a sacrifice is made.

At certain moments, one realizes that a part of the physical essence is being left behind in some space devoid of true life. The divine exists in every particle. People say even in stones, life can be instilled through *Pran Pratishtha* (consecration). Temples and idols are charged with life through this process. Similarly, when constructing a home, we charge it with life. But this can contradict the natural laws of the earth. If you do not live in harmony with these laws, frustration and imbalance arise, affecting not just you but everything around you.

So much mass has accumulated on Earth due to construction. Remember the moment when you worshipped your home—what happens to your list of experiences? The daily impacts you face in life stem from this. Compare the construction of a concrete building with the creation of human life. There's a difference. Human creation has a heart-centered essence, while concrete buildings lack such commitment.

Here's another angle: after the construction of massive projects like the Three Gorges Dam, the Earth's rotation slowed by 0.06 seconds. This change expanded the canvas of our world, contributing to climate change. Over the next six or seven years, this canvas will further expand. This could lead to significant impacts, including population shifts. Children born post-concrete construction seem to carry certain blocked spaces in their physique, while those born earlier had openness in their essence.

Think about it: the body is structured according to universal laws. The rivers, streams, and lakes on

Earth have parallels within our bodies. These constructs impact us deeply. The Three Gorges Dam and other projects have changed Earth's dynamics. When twin towers collapsed, people nearby felt a massive shock—not just from the physical fall but from the spatial disturbance it caused. Similarly, new generations are shaped by these imbalances.

This gap has widened so much that children born in recent years reflect these structural shifts. They carry the weight of the changes in their very being. Concrete construction has had such a massive impact that it is considered cursed by Lord Shankar. He destroyed Tripura because Mayasura, having been blessed, built three grand palaces—one of gold, one of silver, and one of iron. From where did he extract these minerals? The Earth is as alive as our physical bodies. If you were to remove such elements from your body or mine, survival would be impossible. Yet, these elements are extracted from the Earth to create constructions. For the Earth to survive as a planet, these resources must remain intact; otherwise, it leads to an imbalance, like inflammation.

Consider the case of our younger brother, a sanyasi. The inflammation of human physicality ranges from zero to six, with six being the maximum. But what happens when it reaches 200? I asked how 30-32 people entered this scenario, and the answer was that the sanyasi was married but hadn't undergone further spiritual *sanskars*. According to Guruji, there is typically only one head in a house. If concrete construction work is undertaken, it influences not just the physical environment but also the subtle energy and thoughts within that space.

Take, for example, Vastu Shastra. Changes in physical surroundings and thought patterns are linked. You are advised to visit Lord Ram's temple. Why Lord Ram? Ram belonged to the Suryavansha lineage, representing Surya (the Sun), which is full of *Rajoguna* (active energy). Every task—whether aligned with truth or not—requires strength. Truth means following the laws of nature. If you protect these laws, you earn virtue (*Punya*), which aligns with *Dharma*. Dharma is the law of the Earth, and its enforcer is Yamaraj. If you uphold Dharma, it leads to virtuous deeds (*Satkarma*), enabling survival.

However, breaking these laws is a sin and leads to destruction. All sages in Sanatan Dharma emphasized the importance of living in harmony with these laws during one's lifetime on Earth. Even following the truth requires *Rajoguna*. That's why Ram is worshipped. Similarly, Krishna, who represents mastery over the senses, is revered.

Dasharath, Ram's ,father, symbolizes control over the ten senses. When the senses become difficult to manage, you turn to Krishna for guidance.

The scriptures explain this through stories, such as that of Mayasura, who constructed Tripura and was ultimately destroyed by Shankar. Mayasura also built the Maya Sabha for the Pandavas, where Draupadi mocked Duryodhan, saying, "The son of a blind man is blind." Though harsh, she was truthful. Dhritarashtra, Duryodhan's father, symbolized blindness—not just physical but spiritual. Gandhari, Dhritarashtra's wife and Shakuni's sister, chose to blindfold herself in solidarity.

The Mahabharata illustrates deeper truths about creation. Dhritarashtra's 100 sons, including Duryodhan and Dushasan, represent negative tendencies. Similarly, Mayasura's descendants, including Dundubhi and Mandodari, symbolize various aspects of the physical and subtle worlds. Scriptures like the Bhagwat further elaborate on these themes, linking them to *Rajoguna* and virtuous actions.

Mayasura's constructions, such as Maya Sabha, also highlight the impact of creating physical structures on human life. Draupadi's assembly hall led to Duryodhan's humiliation. The act of construction involves sacrifices—of elements, resources, and energies. When this is done against the natural order, it impacts future generations. For example, the orientation of a house (east-facing, Ishan, or Agni directions) influences physical and mental well-being. Without proper understanding, such constructions affect not only individuals but also their children.

In this process, the spouse plays a crucial role in maintaining balance. Their connection to the children sustains the family's health and stability. This topic ties back to *aahuti* (offerings)—whether of resources or the sapta dhatus (seven bodily elements). Intelligent intercourse, for example, involves the use of these elements. Each sacrifice made in the act of creation, whether physical or structural, leaves an impact.

Consider the example of Mukesh Ambani's child's grand marriage. Such events reflect the culmination of material construction, symbolic of modern-day rituals tied to physical and societal structures. These influences extend to every aspect of life, whether spiritual or material. Understanding and aligning with natural laws is the key to navigating these dynamics.

More than three percent—one-third—is not his son. Mukesh Ambani himself provided that support. His son received support from his mother, and she supported

Mukesh Ambani in the construction process. This isn't just a matter of timing. If you have any questions, please share your comments.

Nikita: Yes, Swami Ji. Is everything clear to the participants? Please ask your questions. Pankaj, please proceed.

Pankaj: Pranam, Swami Ji. You have spoken extensively and provided a fresh perspective on Vastu, connecting it beautifully to human psychology, life, and the dynamics of male and female energy. My heartfelt gratitude for your insights. My question is this: due to my busy schedule, the house I bought is a builder-made, ready-to-move property.

I currently live in Dehradun, the capital of Uttarakhand. When I moved here for work, I initially lived in a rented house. Later, I purchased a flat. After some time, I sold that flat and bought a duplex house, which is also a builder's property. Builders often market their properties as "Vastu-compliant," but despite this, I feel that certain issues persist in my life.

For example, while I am growing professionally and positionally, my financial growth seems stagnant. I wonder if this could be due to the Vastu of the builder flat. Could you please provide guidance on this?

Swami Ji: You see, when someone experiences stagnation, particularly in financial matters, it often indicates a sense of incompleteness. The reason behind this is a lack of awareness about what you are receiving. Vastu, as a concept, hasn't been fully understood or integrated.

When you live in such properties, there is often a rhythm or harmony that is missing. This creates dissatisfaction with your day-to-day life—not to the extent that you want to abandon your home and run away, but there is avoidance of facing your current reality.

The core issue is that concrete construction should not dominate your thoughts, even for a few minutes, when considering Vastu. Think of the process as similar to wearing a gold chain or ring—your sacrifice is encapsulated within the gold, and the process is complete. In ancient scriptures, women were advised to wear a yellow thread as part of this principle.

During the Mahabharata and Ramayana periods, Vastu principles were deeply rooted in natural law. Dwarka, for instance, submerged; Lanka, built with immense wealth, was eventually looted. However, construction was permitted for those aligned with Rajoguna (a quality representing action and energy). Kings, as ultimate embodiments of Rajoguna, could create within forts without issue.

Today, even when you purchase a scooter, you perform rituals like Dussehra worship, which essentially involve invoking Bhairava energy. Bhairava worship involves certain offerings like white flowers and camphor to maintain balance. This concept applies similarly to the gadgets or devices you bring into your home—they require their own rituals and interactions.

When living in a rented house, you perform Grihapravesh (housewarming) and symbolically compensate the owner with money. Money, being Rajoguni, becomes a means of solving problems in today's world. However, the exchange of money alone doesn't resolve the underlying Vastu connection, especially when dealing with builder properties.

In duplex apartments or societies, the land's Bhoomi Pujan (groundbreaking ritual) is performed collectively, but each individual owner is still connected to the builder who initiated the construction. This builder, in essence, holds the primary Vastu energy, and your financial transactions act as compensatory sacrifices.

Thus, the stagnation you feel could stem from the incomplete energy transfer or imbalance inherent in such builder-based constructions. You are the fittest individual in your family, but your wife may have her own unique perspectives or approaches. Meanwhile, your children may be facing challenges or difficulties, and they are, in a way, compensating for the emptiness or gaps in your life.

In essence, you are trying to balance yourself, but they are not entirely aligned with or ready for you. This reflects your current situation, and it's a story unfolding within your family dynamics.

Mr. Pankaj, before making any decisions, think carefully about what I have conveyed. I have answered your question two or three times, but the clarity of my message may not have fully come through yet. What I want to communicate is important, so reflect on it deeply.

Pankaj: Swami ji, I have a small question. You mentioned earlier that when we register a house in our name and perform the Grihapravesh Puja, it is like offering a form of monetary compensation and making it ours. However, when I bought my third house, a flat, the situation was different. The builder had marketed it as an investment opportunity and promised it could be rented out immediately. Due to time constraints, I couldn't perform any puja on that property before the tenant moved in. Does this create any issues or complications? Does not offering a dakshina or performing rituals impact the property or us?

Swami ji: Pankaj ji, your question brings up an important point. If we look at this from a broader perspective, how many people in India or globally perform Vastu Puja? If we exclude those following Hindu practices, the percentage is minimal. This desire for construction and ownership stems from a human right to create and possess, which has been ingrained in us for ages.

Now, coming to your specific case, this is not just about one property but three. What is your better half's name?

Pankaj: Sangeeta Mishra.

Swami ji: Okay, now let's reflect for a moment. Sangeeta Mishra, are you listening? As a Brahmin, certain responsibilities are expected of your lineage, and this connection to rituals and dharma cannot be ignored. Pankaj ji, you've already made your decisions and moved forward, but there are still remedies to align your actions with the energies around you.

Let me add a perspective from the story of Lord Ram. When Sita Mata was exiled, an Ashwamedha Yagya was to be performed. However, as Sita was absent, her idol had to be installed. The sculptor crafted many idols, but none resonated with Ram ji until one statue embodied her essence. It was only then that the idol was consecrated, and the yagya could proceed. This highlights the significance of intention, ritual, and alignment in every action.

Similarly, in your case, the property may not have received the ritual consecration or connection, and its energy remains incomplete. The act of giving dakshina or performing puja is not just ceremonial but symbolic of bringing harmony to the space.

Pankaj: Swami ji, I understand. There's no issue with the sound or the message, and your words are clear. I'll reflect on this. Thank you for your guidance.

Swami ji: Good. Returning to Ramayana, this connection to space and energy is vital. The Ashwamedha Yagya represents the flag of knowledge and spiritual completion. These concepts are misunderstood and often taken literally. Knowledge from the Vedas, such as Samveda, Rigveda, and even Ramayana, speaks of a profound connection with nature and the cosmos. The essence of creation is about harmonizing with the energies of the earth and its elements.

In your case, the lack of ritual or alignment may have left the property in a state of imbalance. While this may not create immediate visible issues, it does affect the harmony and flow of energy in your life. Remedies can still be performed to align the space and bring balance to your endeavors. Ram Sukhdas Ji Maharaj, before his passing, instructed that no photos of him should be kept. He believed in simplicity and detachment, as seen in places like Shantikunj Haridwar or Rishikesh's

Swargashram, which were built with a focus on spiritual practice rather than material attachment.

Maharaj often spoke about how modern tools, like a stick in earlier times or a mobile phone today, are given to us for convenience but end up consuming our lives. If we truly wish to act with purpose, we should use these tools wisely and, when no longer needed, return them or pass them on.

The essence of his teaching was understanding and living in harmony with the laws of nature. On a mass level, practices like *Pran Pratishtha*—the act of instilling life energy into objects—have become more symbolic than meaningful. For example, people incorporate such practices even in modern items like wristwatches. This highlights how we seek spiritual connection in mundane things.

Changing clothes twice a day, Maharaj humorously remarked, ensures something remains with the body, making things easier at the time of one's funeral. Otherwise, life and its questions disappear as quickly as a fleeting moment. His sanyasi humor underscores the impermanence of material concerns and the need to focus on what truly matters.

This leads us to the question of how these principles apply to the modern context, especially concerning humanity's relationship with animals and nature. It's an open discussion, inviting reflection on how spiritual teachings can address the challenges of today's world.

Pankaj: Swami ji, earlier you mentioned that Vastu defects might not be a hindrance. However, when we experience life changes, such as changing jobs, can Vastu-related issues in our current house still have an impact?

Swami ji: There is no Vaastu defect, but your thoughts and actions resemble those of Mayasura. Previously, it was advised that you approach Ram to increase Rajoguna (the quality of passion and activity) while decreasing the dominance of the mind. If your goal is to further diminish the mind's influence, you should turn to Krishna, as his path aligns with such spiritual growth. Worshipping a deity (DT) connected to Maya will shape your thoughts accordingly, leading to a complex situation.

As a Brahmin, you should be able to comprehend the solution, though it may seem challenging. The role of a Brahmin, also known as Bhudev (lord of the earth), is to understand the pain of the land. Who else, if not a Sanyasi (renunciate), can do this? For example, a mango tree—known for its Rajoguni qualities—is planted when a child is born, as it symbolizes vitality. In ancient traditions, a mango tree is linked to Rajoguna and has specific significance.

A humorous anecdote illustrates this: A 70-80-year-old man, while walking in a field, encountered a youth. The youth asked him about his calm demeanor despite the hardships of age and remarked on the passing of his seventh wife. The elderly man replied that he might even marry an eighth. The youth, surprised, asked how he remained so vigorous at such an age. The old man attributed his vitality to eating mangoes daily during mango season, emphasizing their strength-giving properties. Such anecdotes highlight the mango tree's significance.

However, Vaastu Shastra advises against planting mango trees within the courtyard of a house, citing potential defects. It is recommended to plant them outside the house boundary, particularly in the southeast direction, near the Agnikon (fire corner). This practice ensures a balanced influence of Rajoguna, preventing misdirection while strengthening positive traits. These guidelines stem from the profound thought processes embedded in spiritual traditions.

For instance, interpreting the Mahabharata reveals cultural parallels, such as countries like China, where societal structures resemble the rule of Dhritarashtra. In such places, there is no practice of Shraddha Tarpan (ancestral rites).

A Brahmin's understanding extends to the nurturing process of a child. For the first four years, a child's mother's "armor" (protection and sanskar) is pivotal. Sages historically refrained from holding children under four, allowing the mother to imprint foundational values. In Rajasthan, traditions like Gangaur worship, which honor Ganesha and Gauri, embody this principle. These rituals align with deeper spiritual practices.

When a child turns five, the mother symbolically passes her protection to the father. This is expressed through the tradition of the child sitting on the father's right thigh, signaling the transfer of the mother's sanskar to the father's guidance. Observing this, the father provides the first initiation, marking a profound moment in the child's spiritual journey.

This is why the father is regarded as the first Guru and the mother as the first deity. Shrimad Shankaracharya, also known as Aadya (the primal teacher), emphasized the significance of the father providing the first initiation, known as the Guru Mantra. This initiation spans eight years, divided into two phases of four years each. The concept of dividing time into these four-year periods reflects a subtle spiritual analysis.

For instance, consider the act of blinking—something that happens in less than a second. According to the Surya Siddhanta, time is so finely measured that a second can be divided into 3,750 subtle parts. This depth of observation demonstrates the intricacies of ancient wisdom. Although we won't delve too deeply into such details here, the spiritual journey unfolds systematically: after four years, the mother's protective "armor" begins to fade. After eight years, the father's armor is relinquished. By the ninth year, the child begins to experience the symbolic influence of their great-grandparents.

Every human being, whether male or female, regardless of lineage, is intricately connected to the elements of this land. For instance, the human body, like the Earth, contains approximately 70% water. In females, this percentage rises to 77%. To balance this excess, cultural practices like piercing ears and noses were introduced. Adorning females with earrings and nose rings symbolically reduced the water percentage, compensating for this imbalance. This connection also ties into the biological role of chromosomes: the XX chromosomes in females are receivers, while the XY chromosomes in males are givers.

Yantra worship reflects this balance through patterns resembling butterfly wings, symbolizing harmony and equilibrium. However, these ancestral practices have diminished over time. Ideally, ancestral influences should fade after 12 to 13 years. Yet, in many cases, these influences linger due to incomplete or neglected rituals. Without performing the proper sanskars (spiritual rites), the ancestors continue to exert their presence.

Today, even in India, such practices are often neglected. Priests fail to emphasize these spiritual traditions, and outside India, they are almost entirely forgotten. For example, societal systems in countries like China resemble the unchecked desires of figures like Duryodhan and Dushasan from the Mahabharata.

The story of Gautam Rishi blessing Indra offers another layer of insight. He blessed Indra with "100 bhag," representing 100 forms of enjoyment and fulfillment. This refers to the completeness of the human experience, symbolized through 100 yantras.

If we delve into these ancient stories and symbols, we find profound connections to the physical and spiritual aspects of life. However, the neglect of these traditions has disrupted the balance between individuals, their ancestors, and their spiritual paths.

The proper sanskars (spiritual rites) have not been performed, leaving the ancestors to influence decisions, as no one seems to care. Even in India, where such traditions were once deeply respected, people have largely stopped paying attention. Priests, who were once responsible for guiding these practices, are no longer addressing them adequately. As for other countries, such as China, the situation is even more disconnected from these traditions. There, societal systems and unchecked desires can be compared to the behaviors of Duryodhan and Dushasan from the Mahabharata.

Sandeep Ji shared an insight about how modern developments have impacted life. For example, the construction of massive structures like the Three Gorges Dam has altered the Earth's natural rhythm, even slowing its rotational speed. This has caused discomfort for the older generation, who were born before these changes occurred. The current generation faces a stark challenge: they must either adapt to these changes or perish.

As time progresses, it seems inevitable that traditions and natural balances will continue to shift. When we look at individuals—male or female—everything eventually falls upon the mother. She bears the burden of responsibility, both physical and emotional. The question arises: how much can a mother endure?

The attack is directed at the mother, and it is coming through some human means. It has become necessary to remove her protective shield.

The father resides on the right side of every human being, while the sisters occupy the center. Each individual is given tasks and expectations—like becoming an MBBS doctor or pursuing ambitions such as becoming an IPS officer. These pressures and frustrations build up as people strive to excel, some even topping their state or achieving success abroad. Yet, after all this, many surrender to disillusionment, realizing the futility of these pursuits. It often culminates in feelings of detachment or *vairaag* (dispassion).

For instance, when someone visits the crematorium to shoulder a bier, they may reflect and say, "All of this is just *Moh Maya* (illusory attachments)." Doctor Pankaj, or rather Pankaj Kumar, if even you feel that life's timing is a mere illusion, it becomes a way to escape. I mentioned this to Sandeep Ji as well. He is a 52-year-old man, and he said, "In two years, I too will leave everything behind, just like you."

Pankaj: Sir, the land that belonged to Ram, Krishna, and Kabir was once the foundation of our immense knowledge. Our Indian knowledge system was so rich. The sages followed a tradition of wisdom, and there was a process of learning through the Upanishads. But after the attacks on great centers of knowledge like Takshila and Nalanda, many libraries were destroyed, and some books were burned.

Despite this, we still became literate and developed over time. Today, India is progressing toward becoming a developed nation. As an educationist myself, I ask: how can we restore the richness of our knowledge system in modern times?

Swami Ji: It is only through the Brahmin and because of the Brahmin that such things happen. This is the power of the Brahmin. Take Chanakya, for example—yes, he was a Brahmin. Do you know why he untied his *shikha* (a tuft of hair traditionally kept by Brahmins)? The *shikha* symbolizes self-control, and its purpose is to ensure that one's vitality, symbolized by sperm, is not wasted unknowingly. Sperm resembles an arrow—it is sharp, purposeful, and directional. If you look at the back side of the male organ, it has a V shape pointing downwards, and both sperm and urine discharge in a similar fashion, like an arrow with a tail and three dots. This arrow concept signifies purity and focus.

If a person harbors negative thoughts and uses their "arrow" destructively, they can kill. But if their thoughts are positive, the same arrow can save lives. Chanakya, by untying his *shikha*, symbolically released the arrows of his intellect and strategy. He rejected *Rajoguna* (the qualities of passion and desire), overthrew a king, and placed a shepherd, Chandragupta Maurya, on the throne. This Brahmin became the Guru who guided the kingdom.

Pankaj: Creation and destruction are nurtured in the lap of a teacher. What a profound statement Chanakya made!

Swami Ji: That's not entirely accurate. The key point is that *Rajoguna* was denied. The Brahmin community is unique in this regard. Look at how Chanakya set aside his personal comforts and chose a shepherd to lead. Similarly, why was Shri Krishna admired as a cowherd? It's because he learned the laws of nature and the essence of the Rigveda from observing cows.

The style of singing has its roots in the Vedas. For example, Luv and Kush reached Ayodhya singing the *Ramayana*. Their singing style reflected the *Samaveda*. The *Atharvaveda* is represented by a monkey face, symbolizing action and tantra. The *Yajurveda* is associated with rituals and ceremonies, often accompanied by pomp and show. Observe goat and sheep. But look at where this has taken us. People spend so much on these—*Vastu Shastra* and such— they sometimes should take out little time to understand the effort made by Rishis to understand law of planet earth from animals and drafted that in simple text for coming generation. Seven course meal for free. They declared (sages – all of them are bramhins accept Vishwamitra & few others) this was possible under cover of king. King has defended them by all means and so the knowledge too is available. Chanakya rejected this approach. He denied the power of occult, the Sun (symbolizing ego), and the king, who is a representation of *Kshatriya* power.

Manu Rishi passed on the knowledge of the *Manusmriti* to Gautam Rishi, preserving wisdom while rejecting the dominance of *Rajoguna (negative aspect)*. This denial brought suffering to the Brahmin community, which has endured much hardship.

Who benefited from all this? It wasn't the Buddhists but rather Buddha himself. Buddha, originally Siddhartha Gautama, was the son of a king, embodying *Rajoguna* once again. His teachings spread, but their foundation was tied to royal patronage. Today, nine countries have embraced Buddhism entirely, but India has not fully accepted it. Why?

India resisted Buddhism because it was heavily influenced by kings, and the Brahmins rejected such establishments. That's why Shrimad Shankaracharya had to emerge—to revive and restore balance in the Indian spiritual tradition.

Because Buddhism was established by a king, it cannot fully represent *Vinaya* (discipline). This creates challenges, even when there are mistakes. Buddha, Siddhartha, or others who renounced their families, wives, and children to take *sanyas* (ascetic life) embody this flaw. In contrast, *Sanatan Dharma* teaches that one can take *sanyas* while living with one's family, without abandoning responsibilities. Escaping from familial duties, as seen in Buddhism, is its fundamental flaw, and this applies to Siddhartha as well. However, his teachings, rooted in *Rajoguna* (the qualities of passion and activity), remain powerful and irrefutable.

Take, for example, Sandeep Agarwal, who is sitting here and is a Khandelwal. Similarly, Ashok Ji from Raipur is a Marwari and a multi-millionaire. Both follow King Agrasen as their Guru. You know of King Agrasen—he fought in the Kurukshetra war before the Pandavas participated. Afterward, he handed over his kingdom to his children, the princes, and entrusted his daughters with a mathematical matrix. He created two 27x27 matrices—one for numbers and one for letters—etched into their hands. The interpretation of these matrices continues even today. There is a book called *Shri Bhuvalya*, which you can look up on Wikipedia. It contains many formulas, such as one where "Ga" equals three, "P" equals one, and "Bha" equals four, among others. These formulas integrate all the *Upanishads*, *Puranas*, global languages, Ayurveda, and more.

After the war, King Agrasen took *sanyas*, and the Marwari community accepted him as their Guru, recognizing his Kshatriya power. This connection is why the Vaishya community is so prosperous today. Wherever you look, you'll see that the British were able to rule because they aligned with kings. Some kings supported them, and this facilitated their dominance. Similarly, the Parsis prospered in Gujarat because the local king supported them. Many communities, flourished due to the support of Kshatriya rulers.

This is all about physical strength and *Rajoguna*. Even in the context of Vaastu (architecture and settlement), a king builds a fort and governs the settlement within. If someone lives inside the fort, the king declares their protection—ensuring that not even a small dent will come to their head or their belongings. This act of providing protection makes the residents loyal allies of the king.

Apart from sons and daughters, the concept of *Vasudev Kutumbakam* (the world as one family) still applies, even if only 1%. The remaining 99% are unaffected, but the 1% presence of others may cause disturbances. In ancient times, people adhered to the laws of nature and the planet Earth. That was their guiding principle. Isn't that so, Mr. Pankaj?

Pankaj: Yes, sir, absolutely fine, very fine.

Swami ji: Alright, I enjoyed this discussion. It's good to see someone engaging in this way. Miss Khandelwal, if you'd like to conclude or ask something—whether about directions, concrete, construction, or other minerals extracted from the earth—know that these activities are considered under the curse of Shankar (Shiva). Hence, Vaastu (architecture) is often seen as carrying this curse. Afterward, we talk about attributes—qualities associated with worshiping Mayasura, for instance, or recognizing that the soul gives life. Without the soul, the body is just a corpse, but with the soul, the body becomes Shiva.

When you go to a temple of Ram, for example, your worship forms a connection to that energy. Similarly, if you worship Hanuman, you align with his attributes; if you worship Kali, you take on her qualities. It reflects on you and shapes your environment. A community or group gets created around such practices—like alumni of a school who are tied to the *Vaastu* of that school, or college alumni tied to the *Vaastu* of their college. This extends to those connected to a madrasa, temple, or gurdwara. These connections to *Vaastu* form distinctions among human beings.

Moreover, when you extract something from the earth and repurpose it, like wood, there are guidelines to follow. For instance, it's said that wood retains life for 12 years, even after a tree is trimmed. This is why wooden construction is often recommended, and why the Jagannath Temple in Puri serves as a living example of this principle. Sannyasis carry sticks (called *danda*) that are considered to have life. They wear wooden sandals, avoid eating from metal vessels, and choose items imbued with life energy.

If you construct with wood, respect the directions, and offset *Vaastu dosh* (architectural defects) by planting a mango tree—a symbol of *Rajoguna*. A mango bush could also work, but it is less beneficial and weakens the individual. Planting towards the *agnikon* (southeast direction, associated with fire) is advised. Beyond this, do not disrupt the planet's natural rotation and revolution with careless construction, as it could lead to humanity's extinction. Wooden construction is not only admired but also faultless.

Pankaj: Swami ji, the National Education Policy emphasizes integrating the Indian Knowledge System into academics. As the Pro Vice-Chancellor of a university in Saharanpur, Uttar Pradesh, I've noticed a recurring issue—while the intent is good, the execution often falls short. For example, an Arts teacher might be appointed to provide superficial information about the subject, complete a two-credit course, and fulfill formalities. I want to go beyond that and ensure the Indian Knowledge System is authentically revived in our syllabus.

On one hand, technology is advancing rapidly with tools like ChatGPT and new artificial intelligence software, but on the other, we must also restore and honor the Indian knowledge tradition. Swami ji, could you provide some guidance or tips on how to achieve this effectively?

Swami ji: Yes, yes, everything a child learns begins in the womb of the mother. The child interacts there, and this is why the concept of *Shruti* and *Smriti* is highlighted in our scriptures. Even without speaking, the child recognizes their parents while still in the womb, along with their relatives, friends, the surrounding environment, and even sounds. For instance, I once gave an example that if a bullfight happens near a pregnant woman, the child can sense the anger and energy from it. Later, after birth, the child might interact with that kind of sound or express emotions linked to it. The medium changes, but the essence of that interaction remains.

Everything the child learns in the mother's womb shapes their life, just like a fingerprint. For example, Doctor Pankaj, your experiences today, the thoughts you've expressed, are connected to interactions you had while in your mother's womb. Some individuals are fortunate to align with these prenatal influences, while others are not, leading to internal conflicts. This occurs because, in the womb, they may have had a certain inclination or purpose, but their life took a different direction.

For instance, if someone is in a profession like politics but lacks the teachings from the womb to cope with it, they struggle. A doctor's child often becomes a doctor, perhaps in a different branch; a film actor's child, if not acting, may take up choreography or a related field. The teachings in the mother's womb guide them. What are you doing for the betterment of society and Indian culture? This is rooted in understanding that our scriptures emphasize obeying nature. Breaking these laws leads to a list of consequences.

Now, Doctor Pankaj, on which floor are you sitting?

Pankaj: I am on the ground floor, sir.

Swami ji: Are you seated on the ground or a sofa?

Pankaj: On a sofa, sir.

Swami ji: If you sit on the ground, you will feel more comfortable because the sofa puts you in opposition to the law of gravity. If someone is on the first floor, fifth floor, or even the 50th floor of Burj Khalifa, the law of gravity affects them differently. The higher they are, the more they are pulled, and it becomes harder to cope. When explaining this, you can say that some people, like *Mayasura*, violate the law of gravity.

In a seminar, I mentioned how crossing a river symbolizes crossing time. The river represents time, and elements like a cow flowing with the river or a snake within it symbolize the passage of time. When you cross a river, even via a flyover, you metaphorically cross time and achieve a state beyond it, called the timeless state. This state can also be achieved through yogasanas, pranayama, and yoga nidra. But it is challenging to make people understand because their worldly concerns weigh them down.

This understanding is not the result of one generation's work but of many generations. Nature, plants, animals, and birds all follow the laws of nature. The mother's womb is the best place for learning. If you want to groom a child, introduce them to knowledge while they are still in the womb. For example, give books to pregnant mothers to read. If someone misuses this knowledge, they destroy themselves. There's no need to worry about that.

The nature of the child will remain as it is, who may destroy his own parents and others, or a positive soul, who will save and offer salvation to his parents. The only way forward is to groom the child before birth. In today's world, you cannot send everyone to Gurukul, force them to sign up for certain teachings, or prevent them from boarding planes. But at the very least, when traveling or working, people should ground themselves.

For example, like Shri Krishna crawled on his knees while stealing butter, we should also crawl at least once daily to stay connected to the ground. There is much more to explore in this direction. Let me know if you have other questions.

Pankaj: I think Gupta wants to do something.

Swami ji: Okay, fine. Can I have a glass of water, please?

Gupta: As long as your water is coming, my concern is that the child who was supposed to be nurtured has already been shaped. Swami ji, he came to me after completing his 12th grade. Now, as I teach him in college, he is entering the first year of B.Tech. or B.Sc. Graduation. He's already developed values and his own ideology. Now, my task is to nurture him further, help him become an employed graduate, a good citizen, and also introduce him to the Indian knowledge system. This is where the challenge lies. If more educators like you join our group—many professors and doctorate holders—I believe we can integrate the Indian knowledge system. We can talk about Aryabhata, Chanakya, and even in our syllabus, we're teaching material like the Kailash Chawla McLaren series. You're a learned person in mathematics too. So, do you think integrating the Indian knowledge system would be beneficial for the children?

Swami ji: Of course! You see, these children are with you for four to six hours a day, and you have the entire year to guide them. This water, you should make it mandatory in your class. Every student should carry a bottle of water. After each class, ask them to drink water. After each teaching session, whether from you or your colleagues, make sure to do this. *Sahana vavtu sahnau bhunaktu, sah viryam (semen) karvaha*– along these lines, you'll notice that these water molecules will absorb your energy. If we use plastic bottles, the photons won't pass through, and the electrons won't ignite. But if we use metal bottles, the students will resonate with your energy. There will be a healthy competition in your class. The students above ninety percent will push each other to perform better. Nobody will fall behind. They'll even compete in exams, striving to be better. This is a simple solution. If you're guiding your child, have a conversation with them for two hours alone, or talk to your wife alone, keep a glass of water after the conversation. Have them drink, and you should drink too. You'll see, during tests and evaluations, such changes will happen. This is the simplest approach. Tell me another model, Pankaj ji.

Swami ji: So, will you have some water?

Pankaj: Yes.

Swami ji: Miss Khandelwal, anything else?

Nikita: Yes, Swami ji, what you told me, I wasn't aware of those things. I'm truly grateful for the opportunity to be here and learn from you, like many others...

Swami ji: We're also happy, Nikita. You listened patiently, and we didn't even realize how many hours had passed.

Nikita: Regarding the bottles, we usually thought we should avoid plastic, but now I understand why we should choose metal. You've explained these small things, and even the idea of growing mango plants is really nice. But Swami ji, I think I'd like to request the participants, if any of you have any special queries or questions like this, please feel free to ask because this is a golden opportunity. When else will you get a chance to ask Swami ji?

Nikita: Participants, we have solved some of Pankaj ji's queries today, which were on our minds too, but we had taken them lightly. Today, we're going to learn the real solutions, which are very genuine. So, I would request the participants to also bring forward any such queries they might have.

Pankaj: Nikita, I'm joining now. Could you please tell us something about Swami ji, where is he from, his contact number, or any other contact information? I am also a professor at a university, so if I ever need to contact him, it would be helpful.

Nikita: Speaking of Vastu, Swami ji, I also have a question. I want to plant a banana tree and a cactus tree in front of my house. What is the main reason behind this?

Swami ji: The banana tree is good, it's always good for taking care of your mind. It's not about Rajoguna but about controlling your mind. Rajoguna leads to better life, but if Rajoguna becomes too dominant, then the banana tree compensates for it. However, the banana tree shouldn't be too close to the house because it compensates repeatedly and brings things down. Also, thorny trees should be avoided. People may keep roses, but cactus should not be there because it grows in the region of Saturn. It increases your desires. Well, desire is essential for a person. Our bodies are made to fulfill desires. If there are no desires in you, it's like not having the desire for food—look at animals. Desire is natural and part of nature's law, so you should always keep that in mind. Thorny trees enhance your desires, so they should not be kept. They also take away your rajoguna, will also make you weak. For example, if you study under an acacia tree, it turns into something negative. It's said that guests should be made to sleep in the Vayu angle so they leave quickly. But why should they leave? They're guests—let them stay in the house. The guest angle is actually the Agni angle, the Mars angle, and if you place anything there, it gets enhanced. For instance, if you make that space a bedroom for a couple, it will enhance their chances of having children. We met someone during our recent visit to Ahmedabad. In Gujarat, there's a place called Ranpur, where we stayed at a farmhouse. It was located in a remote area, and we stayed there for a few days. The person who owned the place was a Brahma Kumari, a Sadhika who had been a Brahma Kumari for 35 years. She was not in the traditional Brahma Kumari attire, but she had taken sannyas and led a solitary, ascetic life. She had previously taken sannyas at the age of 15 and sometimes received invitations from home for events like weddings. She would still eat food from the ashram and had many shoes, which she kept in the fire corner.

She used to travel a lot, going to places like Ahmedabad, Gandhinagar, Porbandar, Rajkot, and she even hosted other sadhus at her farmhouse. She was very devoted to the ascetic lifestyle. We stayed for three weeks, just before the Chaturmas, which was very hot. During this time, I told her to move her shoes from the fire pit and place them aside so that she could keep something more useful there. I advised her that keeping gold, silver, or a bank passbook in the fire angle would bring positive outcomes, but keeping shoes there was unnecessary as it only symbolized travel.

I also shared that sleeping under an acacia tree could be harmful, as it develops desires, but desires are essential for a human body. On other hand salvation too is desire and to attain Nirvana the thought of that too is not execpted as it falls under desire. The banana tree, on the other hand, helps control the mind. I mentioned a simple way to control the mind, like brushing your teeth in the morning, cleaning your "10 gates," and maintaining cleanliness to keep your mind calm and focused. The "10th gate" is a spiritual concept that relates to the first seed of the father, which is said to be removed after four years. The seed represents a connection to divinity and spiritual practices.

In discussing spiritual concepts, I mentioned the importance of Satvik qualities, symbolized by the letter "Sa," which stands for truth, happiness, respect, and Sanatan Dharma. The idea is to live in harmony with the laws of nature, following the Yama Niyama (moral codes) of this planet. People should live happily, without hate or animosity. The sages of India are revered for their wisdom, and their teachings reflect respect for nature and the universal laws that govern life.

Vivek: Swami Ji, I would like to say that Ajay Rao Ji, who are very deep experts in Vastu is with us. I would like to invite Ajay Rao Ji to share his thoughts, please.

Ajay Rao: Thank you, thank you. It's an honor to be present here. Swami Ji, you mentioned a lot that is in line with the scriptures, and I got a new perspective from what you shared. I have been involved with Vastu since childhood, as my father was also into it. He passed away recently, and for me, Vastu is as natural as breathing, like Pranayam—it's a part of my very being. So, you've given me a new way to think about it. Thank you so much.

Vivek: Oh, we also have Manish Poonia Ji, who is in real estate and is from Dehradun. He's online, so kindly share your views, please. Okay, okay, I can be offline too. Swami Ji, please continue.

Swami Ji: Is there anything left to say? Please, if there's something, feel free to tell us. We can talk about Vastu. Yes, regarding what Japan has mentioned, the type of construction they describe, using bamboo wood, I don't know the specific name for it, but that's what I want to say. If a creature is present in such a structure, it doesn't fall under Vastu Dosh. If you want to dig a pit down to Talatal, then you need to conquere Mayasura in Sapta Patal. Otherwise, with wood, I think I have answered your question, Kapil, right?

Vivek: Swami Ji, I'll interrupt for a moment. Dr. Sadanand Tripathi Ji, a great scholar of Sanskrit, is also with us. If he wants to say something, please, please, please, go ahead. I'm recording, please continue.

Nikita: Sadanand sir, would you like to express something? Hello, yes sir, you're audible, please go ahead.

Sadanand: Yes, sir, Swami Ji, respectful pranam.

Swami Ji: Hari Om!

Sadanand: Namo Namah. I would like to ask about the origin of the word Vastu. How do we understand its beginning? What is the origin of the word Vastu in both the animate and inanimate worlds?

Swami Ji: You've heard about this from the beginning.

Sadanand: I've been connected with you from the beginning. There's a lot of confusion being spread about the concept of the word Vastu.

Swami Ji: If you talk about Dhatu (element), what does it mean if we break the sandhi (compound)? It means Amrit Beej (immortal seed), something beyond this. Something beyond this, Sadanand Ji.

Sadanand: Tell me, tell me, Acharya Ji, tell me.

Swami Ji: Is this enough? In the sutras, is this enough that it is Amrit Beej?

Sadanand: No, this has become a seed, that has become a seed.

Swami Ji: Creation is only possible from Amrit (immortal essence). *Van Amrit tatvatmikaye (Vam letter stands for sector- amrit).* That Amrit element is not a physical body, it's liquid *(ark)*. Now, consider this: That object, which we pronounce as Ka, Kaa, Kha, Ga, Gha, has its end in Vastoo. But the object itself is not Vastu. Even if you call the object an idol, you're still performing Pran Pratishtha (the process of infusing life into it). Or, after a yajna, the hut is burned after completing the rituals, and it is said, "Idam Na Mam" (This is not mine). Establishment is only possible from Amrit, Sadanand Ji. Whether it's Vastu in the form of

Pindi or building a house or any Vastoo (goods), the important point is this: If you want to build a house, try to use wood. If you cannot do that, as I mentioned earlier, plant a mango tree at birth. A mango tree has Rajoguna (a quality of activity), and when a person reaches 80-90 years of age, the same age as the tree, the wood of the mango tree is used for the funeral pyre because Marut (wind element) resides in the mango tree. The departed soul, in its last life, listens to Marut and reaches its destination. At birth, a person should plant a mango tree so that their Aayush (lifespan) is nourished. But they should not only eat mangoes for four months, as I told you in the story, because that would create an imbalance. This is why the mango tree is beneficial for everyone. It provides forward movement, even after birth and death. In Sanatan Dharma, we have a beautiful method of handling the body's Vastu after death. When the body becomes a corpse, there is no soul in it, and if the body is not in a state of wellness, it should be cremated. After cremation, the body should be done with Rajoguna, using mango wood. That's why Ram's name is chanted in the crematorium, as Ram's name represents Rajoguna. The idol of Shankar is also placed there because, if there are any imperfections or blockages in the deceased's journey in the other world, Shankar's idol helps to remove them. The funeral is performed with the branches and wood of a mango tree, which helps the soul progress. The remains are then immersed in a river, giving the soul further movement, following a 16-day ritual to ensure the person's Vastu is cleared.

Now, if the Vastu of the body is made of concrete, it must be demolished. If this cannot be done, then the property should be given away to your lineage, so that you become free. Not even a penny should remain from what you established, except for your son and daughter, who will continue your lineage. The thought processes you had at the time of your birth form the seed, and from that seed, your descendants continue their journey. As long as they stay with you and have not formed their own nuclear family, you continue to provide for them. The man's Sun energy is directed downward onto the woman's Sun energy because she carries a child in her womb, and that is why women tend to attract you. This is why men remain cautious, as they may sacrifice enjoyment but gain something greater in return—a son, a daughter, and much more. If a man tells his wife that he wants to become rich, it becomes a miracle, and he does. If the wife adopts the same attitude, she too will be transformed. Isn't this a beautiful statement?

Swami ji : I know Sadanand you have asked Nispatti not uttpatti of Vastu, the construction, end result. Who ever is born has a period of life. Make it or Mar it.

Nikita: Thank you so much, Swami Ji, for sharing somuch with us today. You spoke about the body, soul, and Rajoguna, everything was insightful, and I think all the participants must have really appreciated it. Our whole family is feeling very happy to have you on this platform.

Swami Ji: Thank you, Vivek Bajpai. We were meditating in solitude by the banks of the Narmada when they found us. Thank you to everyone for listening so patiently, and the questions were excellent. Nikita Ji, thank you as well. We enjoyed it.

Nikita: Thank you, and thank you to all the participants for being cooperative and attentive listeners. It's been great. Hari Om, Swami Ji.

Swami Ji: Hari Om, Hari Om!

www.ingramcontent.com/pod-product-compliance
Ingram Content Group UK Ltd.
Pitfield, Milton Keynes, MK11 3LW, UK
UKHW040857240225
455493UK00001B/44

9 789367 830437